COASTAL VESSELS
A Colour Portfolio

David L. Williams & Richard de Kerbrech

Ian Allan
PUBLISHING

CORNCRAKE *(Previous page)*

(5/1946) General Steam Navigation Co (GSNCo)
640grt; 192ft (58.52m) loa × 32ft 10in (10m) beam
H. Robb, Leith
Oil 4SA 6-cyl by Masch. Kiel AG, Kiel: bhp not known

The *Corncrake* was launched on 20 December 1945 as a sister ship to
GSNCo's *Redstart* for the company's postwar building programme.
Although known by many Londoners as a Thames and English Channel
excursion firm, the GSNCo had a growing fleet of cargo coasters which
by 1966 had risen to some 31 vessels, all named after birds. Unlike other
ships in the company, which were three-hatch centre island, the
Corncrake was a two-island open shelter decker. She was sold in 1967
and renamed *Twillingate*. By 1999 she had been deleted from Lloyd's
Register. This view of her taken in September 1964 shows her under way
on the River Thames.
Kenneth Wightman

First published 2008

ISBN (10) 0 7110 3205 X
ISBN (13) 978 0 7110 3205 7

© Ian Allan Publishing 2008

Published by Ian Allan Publishing

an imprint of Ian Allan Publishing Ltd, Hersham Surrey, KT12 4RG
Printed by Ian Allan Printing Ltd, Hersham Surrey, KT12 4RG

Code: 0801/B1

Visit the Ian Allan Publishing website at www.ianallanpublishing.com

EXPLANATORY NOTES

Preceding each caption or group of captions is a block of technical
and date information relating to the named and featured ship or
ships. The layout of this information, is as follows:

The vessel's name, (month and date of entry into service);
former names with the (year) in which the name changes occurred;
the vessel's owners;
the vessel's vital statistics: tonnage, length and beam in feet and
inches with the equivalent (metric values);
the vessel's builders and shipyard location;
the engine installation, the engine builders and, where known, the
horsepower output.

ABBREVIATIONS

Throughout, the following abbreviations have been adopted:

bp	length between perpendiculars
ft	feet
grt	gross registered tonnage
in	inches
loa	length overall
m	metres
2SA	Two-stroke Single Acting
4SA	Four-stroke Single Acting
bhp	brake horsepower
cyl	cylinders
DR	double reduction
hp	horsepower
ihp	indicated horsepower (a calculated or horsepower, nominally reckoned as 87% of brake horsepower)
LP	low pressure
nhp	nominal horsepower
shp	shaft horsepower
SR	single reduction

Introduction

Like the fine details in an oil painting, it is the myriad of small vessels all around the coast that completes the picture of British shipping. In all their great variety, they bustle in port approaches and work the coastline and tidal rivers the length and breadth of the United Kingdom.

The typical, prewar general cargo steam coaster was immortalised by John Masefield in his famous poem 'Cargoes', in which he evocatively described it as the:

> Dirty British coaster with a salt-caked smoke stack
> butting through the Channel in the mad-March days
> with a cargo of Tyne coal, road-rail, pig-lead,
> firewood, iron-ware and cheap tin trays.

Intensively industrious, hard-working craft, coasters may well have been dirty through the nature of their duties and the heavy demand placed on them – the need to earn continuous revenue versus the limited time for maintenance and being out of service. Moving forward from the time when John Masefield's poem was written to the 1950s and 1960s, the period covered by this book, the cargoes carried may well have changed but only slightly. Coal and scrap iron and construction girders were still being transported, but there was also petroleum and other oil products, sand, lime, aggregates, cement, stone, timber, sewage (sludge), chemicals, fertilizer, grain, vegetables, pulverised coal, liquid natural gas, steel and steel products and even, yes, cherry brandy and Guinness.

In the era covered by this modest volume, a coastal ship was once defined as a vessel which was permitted to trade within Home Trade limits, ie between the River Elbe, Germany, and Brest in north-west France. Outside these limits the ship was then classified as an ocean-going vessel and was required to comply with regulations applicable to this type of ship. While several owners designed their vessels such that they could, with little trouble, engage in longer voyages, thus increasing considerably the possibility of keeping them running with full cargoes, others concentrated their activities on estuarial and adjacent ports and their vessels were rarely, if ever, seen in continental waters. The former, by way of distinction, were referred to as 'short-sea traders'. Latterly, however, it was recognised that there was significant overlap between these types. To quote the well-known maritime writer Frank E. Dodman: 'No hard and fast rule can be drawn between the coaster and the short-sea trader. No particular vessel can, therefore, be identified primarily as a coaster, as the small freighter between 300 and 1,500 gross tons may be on charter (tramping), coasting or carrying cargo on short-sea scheduled service.' In this book we have covered vessels that fall in both these categories as well as craft that could be accurately described, because of their small size, as being exclusively inshore or river vessels.

To emphasise this point, the very nature of coastal shipping and the diverse range of cargoes carried – virtually every commodity imaginable, from the main transhipment ports in Britain and on the Continent to every small harbour, discharge wharf and anchorage throughout the British Isles – imposed a significant measure of specialisation on vessel design. Hence, there was no such thing as the typical 'coaster'. The ships to be found in the coaster class were manifold: from the fast cargo vessels engaged on an intricate network of scheduled services, to those employed on the basis of time or single voyage charters for particular bulk commodities, and the slower and smaller colliers which typically ran year in and year out on the same itinerary, servicing power stations and gas stations alike.

Besides these, many other coastwise-engaged vessels served a wide range of equally vital duties. There were the dredgers, of the grab, bucket and suction types, that kept port channels clear for large merchant ships, as well as the hopper barges that worked in conjunction with them. Alongside the larger cargo vessels were the many small motor barges and lighters, including the unique Clyde 'puffers'. There were the tenders and cutters of the pilotage and lightage authorities, and the salvage and survey ships operated by some of the major port authorities. Coastal tankers were engaged in the transportation of refined oil, bunker fuel for long-distance merchantmen and liquefied gas products from the oil refineries to fuel distribution centres. In the estuaries of the Clyde, Mersey and

Thames special craft were employed carrying city effluents for discharge in deep water. And so on. Within these categories, there were further specialisations. For instance, colliers which, beyond certain basic features (three or four large hatches to facilitate grab discharge and, usually, an absence of cargo-handling gear) were divided into two distinct groups: larger vessels which served down-river installations and had a conventional raised superstructure and those that were known as 'flatirons' or 'flatties', which were virtually devoid of superstructure so that they could pass under London's many low bridges on their way to up-river discharge berths. On the latter, the tall funnels of steam-driven vessels were hinged, while the squat ones on motorships were telescopic, as were their light pole masts.

In the pages that follow there are examples of many of these coastal vessel types, a snapshot view of the British coastal scene from the 1950s continuing into the 1970s.

Coaster evolution up to and beyond the period covered by this volume has reflected the continuing changes to trade patterns, industrial practices, shipbuilding technology and even government subsidisation practices – essentially all those economic influences that have determined whether the shipowner made a profit or a loss.

Back in the days of John Masefield, the coasting ship was typically a coal-fired steamer with either compound or triple expansion steam reciprocating engines and a number of vessels from that period which survived in service in the postwar years are illustrated here. But, as with other merchant ship types, the transition to internal combustion machinery accelerated after the Second World War and the majority of the coastal vessels completed from 1945 onwards had diesel engines. The internal combustion engine particularly suited coasters in which, constrained by their modest dimensions, it was essential to devote the maximum amount of space to revenue-earning cargo. The compactness and relative lightness of the diesel engine, along with the elimination of main boilers, not only freed up valuable space but also meant that vessels' draught could be kept as shallow as possible, allowing access to ports with minimal water depth. Likewise, for up-river craft, this had the benefit of lower air draught for bridge clearance. Furthermore, the advantages of reduced crew numbers and the ability to store fuel in the most

convenient location within the hull, rather than in close proximity to the furnaces, all contributed to the motor engine's appeal.

Just as the adoption of the diesel engine has influenced the external appearance of coastal vessels in general, so too other improvements have changed the look of bulk trade coasters, in particular. Larger hatch openings now have automated steel covers replacing manually-handled wood and canvas. The two-island, midships and aft, accommodation structures have given way to single superstructure blocks, usually located aft, eliminating the wasteful expense of piping hot and cold running water along a greater length of the hull. Cargo holds have had their internal surfaces 'smoothed' by the concealment or elimination of protruding frames in order to facilitate loading, discharge and cleaning. Similarly, on coastal tankers the tanks have been given special linings with acid or alkaline-resistant properties to permit the sequential carriage of fluids that would otherwise be contaminated.

Overall, within the constraints imposed by lock entrances, channel depths or other navigational considerations, coasters of every type have increased in size, substantially raising their cargo-carrying capacity for little or no additional operating cost.

The owners and operators of these coastal vessels, as the backbone of the coastwise trade, were as distinctively known as the big international shipping companies engaged in deep-water trading. Companies like Everards, General Steam Navigation Company, Metcalfs, Cory Maritime, Gibson, Rowbotham, and Comben Longstaff, and many other famous concerns, were once well-known names equally familiar to shipping enthusiasts. It was the same for the various collier-owning gas companies – the nationalised CEGB, NTGB and SEGB – as well as Stephenson Clarke, Hudsons and John Kelly; likewise for Esso Petroleum, Shell Mex and BP Oil, all as renowned for their coastal tankers as they were for their immense crude oil carriers.

Many of these companies have since disappeared, though, because, just as the postwar coastwise scene had changed significantly from that which inspired John Masefield's dedication to the 'dirty British coaster', so too the character of coastal shipping today has changed significantly, bearing only a cursory resemblance to that of 30 to 40 years ago. The advent of the roll-on–roll-off ferry along with an explosion of road haulage in the form of juggernaut trucks, exploiting an improved road infrastructure, has eradicated much of the conveyance of general freight on which the short-sea coaster depended for its living. In the face of such competition the traditional sea-borne trade has drastically decreased. Likewise, the demise of the UK mining industry and the switch from town gas to North Sea (natural) gas has put an end to the coastal colliers. Automation programmes for lighthouses and lightships have meant that their crews could be dispensed with and so too the large fleets of tenders that once serviced these stations. It is much the same for pilot cutters and other coastal craft. The one exception is the coastal tanker which has thrived in the 'age of the car', its numbers having increased in recent times while other coastal types have declined. The continued transport of liquid cargoes of oil, spirit and chemicals by sea rather than by road has suited distributors, probably because of the sheer volumes concerned and the cheaper freight costs.

Finally, it should be mentioned that coastal vessels of all types, by virtue of their operation for a greater amount of the time within port confines or in the busy, restricted waterways of port approaches, have an increased exposure to the risks of collision, navigational hazards and the effects of adverse weather.

We invite the reader to relish the gallery of pictures that follow, revealing a dimension of the shipping scene that is too often overlooked, hidden in the shadows of the exploits of the great ocean ships but which, to this day, remains an essential dimension of port and general maritime affairs. Now little more than the remnants of a once vast coastal shipping fleet, the canvas of the shipping scene seems so much the emptier for the absence of their intrinsic appeal.

As before, we have drawn from the many superb colour photographs taken by Kenneth Wightman and from the collection of slides gathered by Mick Lindsay, the majority seen here for the very first time. It should be noted that some of these views show coasters in more recent times, some under names they adopted well after the mid-1970s, though all these vessels were built prior to 1970 and most of the photographs were taken in the 1960s or earlier.

David L. Williams and Richard P. de Kerbrech
Isle of Wight, April 2007

ACKNOWLEDGEMENTS
Alan Cartwright, Port of London Authority (PLA)
David Clark
Justin Donald, Lloyd's Marine Intelligence Unit
Ron Ellis, National Historic Ships
Mick Lindsay
Michelle Marsden, HM Customs & Excise Museum
Philip Simons & Leslie Spurling, LR Fairplay Limited
Southampton Central Library – Maritime & Special Collections

Our special thanks to Ken Lowe, with his specialist knowledge of coastal vessels, for his guidance and advice.

BIBLIOGRAPHY AND SOURCES
Coast Lines by Norman L. Middlemiss (Shield Publications, 1998)
Comben Longstaff & Co. Ltd. by K.S. Garrett (World Ship Society)
The Dumpy Book of Ships (Sampson Low, Marston & Co, 1957 & 1961)
Ellermans – A Wealth of Shipping by James Taylor (Wilton House Gentry)
Everard of Greenhithe by K.S. Garrett (World Ship Society, 1991)
Fifty Dynamic Years by Richard Cornish, Roy Fenton, Louis Loughran, Richard Osbourne, Joachim Pein and Harry Spong (World Ship Society)
Merchant Ships – various by E.C. Talbot-Booth (Journal of Commerce)
Merchant Ships: World Built – various (Adlard Coles)
Modern Shipping Disasters, 1963–1987 by Norman Hooke (Lloyds of London Press)
Ship Recognition – Merchant Ships by Laurence Dunn (Adlard Coles Ltd)
Ships of the London River by H.M. Le Fleming (Adlard Coles Ltd)
Stephenson Clarke by Craig J.M. Carter (World Ship Society)
Warships of World War II by H.T. Lenton & J.J. Colledge (Ian Allan)

Coastal Ships – various by H.M. Le Fleming or D. Ridley Chesterton (Ian Allan)
Lloyd's Registers
www.miramarshipindex.org.nz
www.clydesite.co.uk/clydebuilt
www.red-duster.co.uk
www.theshipslist.com
www.solentwaters.co.uk

BOLTON

(9/1964) ex *Makurdi* (1973) ex *Else Terkol* (1972)
  ex *Chemitrader* (1965)
Bowker & King Ltd
495grt; 206ft 11in (63.07m) loa × 31ft 7in (9.63m) beam
Fr. Luerssen Werft, Bremen-Vegesack
Oil 2SA 6-cyl by Alpha Diesel A/S, Friedrichshaven: 750bhp

The *Bolton* was originally German-built as a chemical tanker with 18 years prior service. She joined Bowker & King's expanding fleet of 22 coastal tankers which were operated originally on the River Thames, but later over an enlarged sphere of operation. The *Bolton* was still in service with them up until 1985 when she seems to have disappeared from Lloyd's Register. In this view of her taken in July 1977, the *Bolton* is seen moored at Southampton's Town Quay, once a hive of commercial activity. Her high sheer at the forecastle and the flair of the bow above the knuckle betray her early continental design. *Mick Lindsay*

BISLEY

(6/1969) Bowker & King Ltd
701grt; 211ft 1in (64.34m) loa × 30ft 4in (9.25m) beam
R. Dunston (Hessle) Ltd, Hessle
Oil 4SA 8-cyl SR reverse geared by Mirrlees Blackstone
    Ltd, Stamford: 660bhp

When the *Bisley* entered service in 1969 she was the second of a group of six new coastal tankers of similar dimensions, having a deadweight tonnage of around 1,200 to 1,300. These ships were specifically designed for trading to a BP oil depot at Quedgeley on the Gloucester and Sharpness Canal. During the 1970s and 1980s the High Level Bridge at Sharpness was often opened to allow the passage of Bowker & King's coastal tankers. Since the fall off in coastal trade to that port it is now only opened for the occasional excursion vessel. During 1990 she was sold to Mantinia Shipping Co of Piraeus and renamed *Naoussa-Nao 13* and ultimately broken up in Turkey during January 2005. The photograph, taken during May 1984, shows the *Bisley* outward bound from Sharpness. *Mick Lindsay*

BP SCORCHER

(7/1964) ex *Killingholme* (1976) BP Oil Ltd
1,182grt; 214ft 10in (65.49m) loa × 37ft 3in (11.36m) beam
Henry Robb Ltd, Leith
Oil 2SA 6-cyl by British Polar Engines Ltd, Glasgow: 1,230bhp

Originally built for the all motor vessel coastal tanker trade of Shell Mex & BP Ltd, the *BP Scorcher* had a deadweight capacity of 1,420 tons and a speed of 11 knots. When she entered service back in 1964 she was painted in Shell Mex & BP livery and like other vessels in the fleet she could be operated by other companies on charter. Following the break-up of the joint venture with Shell Mex in 1976, leading to the creation of separate coastal operations, BP Oil Ltd was formed to handle BP's share of the trade. In the same year the *Killingholme* passed to the new concern and was renamed *BP Scorcher*. By 1983 she was sold on again to become the *Nigerian Star*. She is seen here at Swansea, photographed on 24 July 1981, only just under way. It would appear that her hull and boot-topping are seriously in need of a paint job. *Mick Lindsay*

BOWCROSS

(8/1967) ex *Chichester Cross* (1971) British Dredging (Shipping) Ltd
968grt; 196ft 1in (59.75m) loa × 39ft 3in (11.97m) beam
Goole Shipbuilding & Repairing Co Ltd, Goole
Oil 4SA 8-cyl SR reverse geared by Blackstone & Co Ltd, Stamford: 1,000bhp

British Dredging (Shipping), which had originally been F. Bowles & Son of Cardiff, operated suction dredgers and sand carriers in London, Bristol and Cardiff, culminating in a fleet of some 13 vessels by 1972. The *Bowcross*, launched on 22 March 1967 as the *Chichester Cross* for John Heaver Ltd of Southampton, was the type of suction dredger that was engaged in the supply of sea-dredged sand and aggregates for the construction industry. One of the *Bowcross*'s consorts was the *Bowbelle* which, on 20 August 1989, was in collision with the excursion vessel *Marchioness* in the River Thames. In 1999 she was sold to R&R Marine Services (Cardiff) for service on the Moroccan coast and renamed *Rita 1*. Here she plied between Tangier and El Jadida for two years before being sold to Meltemi Navigation Co Ltd of Tonga in 2001 and renamed *Captain Spyros*. She was renamed *Kap Spiro* in 2003, probably for her voyage to the breakers. She arrived at Aliaga on 5 February 2003 to be scrapped. This view of the *Bowcross* was taken at Cardiff in June 1972 as she is leaving the basin lock. *Mick Lindsay*

NEEDLES

(1960) British Road Services (BRS)
93grt; ca. 90ft (27.43m) loa × ca. 20ft (6.10m) beam
Richard Dunston, Hessle
2 × Oil 2SA Kelvin: bhp not known

When the motor barge *Needles* joined British Road Services in 1960 she was one of a large fleet of trans-Solent traders that brought goods to the Isle of Wight. She was similar to the later *Northwood* and had a single hold with a heavy lift mast forward. Often, when the hatch was shut and sealed, she shipped vehicles on the hatch itself. Barges like the *Needles* called at Shepards Wharf at Cowes to unload heavy cargoes like tractors and bulldozers before proceeding up the River Medina at high tide to the river's head of navigation at Newport, where BRS had its depot. The *Needles* made her last BRS cargo run to Newport in 1975 after which she found new employment on the west coast of Ireland in support of the fish farming industry there. The British Road Services company continued in existence until 1988 when it disappeared under Government deregulation policies. In this photograph the *Needles* is moored alongside the wharf at Newport, Isle of Wight in February 1965. Resplendent in her BRS colours, it is most likely that she has recently left the nearby Odessa Boatyard slipway where she was freshly repainted. Note the rubber tyres as fenders at her port quarter, a once traditional method of recycling these used items. The building alongside the quay is now the Bargeman's Rest pub. *Ray Sprake*

GRASSENDALE

(10/1954) British Transport Docks Board (BTDB)
677grt; 165ft 11in (50.27m) loa × 34ft 2in (10.42m)
beam
Henry Scarr Ltd, Hessle
Oil 4SA 8-cyl Ruston & Hornsby, Lincoln: 750bhp

The *Grassendale*, which was launched on 31 May 1954, entered service with the British Transport Docks Board of London, along with her sister the *Kenfig*. They were a pair of grab hopper dredgers tasked with dredging dock basins and locks. Although slower and more cumbersome than bucket or suction hopper dredgers, the skill of the operation depended very much on the grab crane driver. A third near-sister, the *Burcom Sand*, entered service in the same year. The undated photograph shows the *Grassendale* alongside at Barrow. The cranes appear huge and unwieldy and must surely have affected the ship's stability when in ballast. The vessel is of the two-island type with a slender structure supporting the bridge and officers' accommodation. *Mick Lindsay*

LAVERNOCK

(7/1967) British Transport Docks Board (BTDB)
1,864grt; 250ft 2in (76.23m) loa × 48ft 6in (14.79m) beam
Ferguson Bros Ltd, Port Glasgow
2 × Oil 4SA 16-cyl driving 2 generators connected to 2 electric motors by Davey, Paxman & Co Ltd, Colchester: 2,200shp

The *Lavernock* was launched on 30 March 1967 and registered in Cardiff. Diesel electric propulsion was chosen for her machinery as it was felt that this was better for manoeuvrability when suction dredging. She had a deadweight capacity of 2,100 tons. She was sold in 1992 to the Bangkok Port & Dredging Company and renamed *Nisarutn* but seems only to have been deployed by them for about two years for she no longer appeared in Lloyd's Register from around 1994. The photograph was taken in October 1979 alongside an unidentified location. From her condition it appears that she has been constantly employed to the detriment of her paintwork, although her suction gear looks to be in good working order. *Mick Lindsay*

The large, powerful grab hopper dredger *Aberavon* served at Cardiff from 1969 under the port's original owners, British Transport Docks Board, and from 1984, following privatisation, for Associated British Ports (ABP). She is seen anchored in the approaches to Cardiff with Penarth Head beyond, the two cranes on her starboard side fully deployed. Towards the stern, one of her lifeboats has been swung out and is being secured alongside. A more modern type of dredging vessel, the *Aberavon* was fitted with doors in the bottom of her hull to permit rapid gravity discharge in deep water. She was sold in 1991, serving Portuguese owners based at Funchal for the next seventeen years as the *Conico*. Thought to be still active, she was sold for a second time in 2006 when her name was shortened to *Nico*. *Mick Lindsay*

ABERAVON

(6/1969) British Transport
  Docks Board (BTDB)
2,113grt; 251ft 2in
  (76.54m) loa × 50ft 2in
  (15.30m) beam
Ferguson Bros, Port
  Glasgow
2 × Vee Oil 4SA reverse
  reduction-geared by
  English Electric Diesels
  Ltd, Paxman Eng. Div,
  Colchester: 3,000bhp

TOWARD LASS

(1942) ex *C.173* (1963) ex
VIC 12 (1947) W. Burke
96grt; 66ft 9in (20.34m) loa
× 18ft 6in (5.64m) beam
Goole Shipbuilding &
Repairing Co Ltd, Goole
Diesel engine: bhp not known

Originally constructed during the Second World War as a VIC (Victualling Inshore Craft) cargo lighter for the Ministry of Shipping, the *Toward Lass* was subsequently acquired by the Admiralty to service warships at base anchorages and naval dockyards, re-identified as the *C.173*. She and her class mates followed the design of the original Clyde puffers immortalised in the tales of Captain Para Handy and his vessel *Vital Spark* and, like them, the *Toward Lass* originally had her funnel ahead of her bridge. In later vessels, this arrangement was reversed and she was herself modified after conversion to diesel propulsion, as illustrated here, berthed with another former VIC vessel, the *Colonsay* ex *VIC 84*. One of 86 such VIC craft originally powered by a simple steam plant, they did not 'puff' however, as their engine was fitted with a condenser. Like so many former VIC craft, the *C.173* was sold for mercantile service in the coasting trade in 1963, acquired by W. Burke & Co of Greenock. It was at this time she received the name *Toward Lass*. The *Toward Lass* was broken up at Dalmuir from February 1980. *Mick Lindsay*

13

ROMARK

(1957) ex *Bergmann* (1975)
Castleville Transport (Pelham Dale & Partners Ltd)
426grt; 171ft 5in (52.25m) loa × 28ft 1in (8.54m) beam
C. Luhring-Brake
Oil 4SA 6-cyl by Masch. Kiel AG: 360bhp

Built as the *Bergmann* for Norwegian owners in 1957 for the carriage of general cargo, with two large derricks, she is typical of those Dutch and German coasters that pioneered the short-sea and cross-channel trade. She passed to the Brighton owners Castleville Transport in 1975 and was renamed *Romark*. In 1985 she was sold to the Tamar Shipping Co Ltd of St Vincent & the Grenadines. Her ownership later passed to the Cassamar Shipping Co in the same locality. As of 2005/06 she was still in service. This view of her moored alongside at Great Yarmouth in July 1978 shows her loading scrap metal. The two dockside cranes in the background appear to be busy. *Mick Lindsay*

GRAINVILLE

(4/1951) ex *Battersea* (1981) Alba Shipping Ltd.
1,777grt; 280 ft 4in (82.45m) loa × 39ft 6in (12.04m) beam
S.P. Austin & Son, Sunderland
Oil 2SA 8-cyl Sulzer: 1,280bhp

Originally built as the collier *Battersea* for the Central Electricity Generating Board (CEGB), the *Grainville* was one of a postwar type of six motor driven 'flatirons' to join the fleet between 1947 and 1951, each with a deadweight capacity of 2,710 tons. As with other colliers of her type, her masts and funnel were built so that they could be lowered for passage under Thames bridges. She was sold to Alba Shipping Co of Cork in 1981 and renamed *Grainville*, as a hint of her new cargo-carrying role. In this photo she is seen laid up alongside at Sunderland on 1 June 1981. There appears to be no life on board, although her MacGregor hatches are open as if ready to work cargo. Note the square section funnel, an unusual feature of the day but later adopted by her builders on the SD14 cargo ship. Ironically this may well be one of the last photographs taken of the *Grainville* for on 14 December 1981 she capsized and sank in position 52°03'N, 06°12'W, some 10 miles off Rosslare, near the Tuskar Rock Light, with the loss of four lives, among them her master. At the time, she was bound from Belfast to Bilbao with a cargo of scrap metal. *Mick Lindsay*

JAMES ROWAN

(6/1955) CEGB
  (Stephenson Clarke)
2,947grt; 340ft 1in
  (103.64m) loa × 43ft
  6in (13.25m) beam
Hall, Russell & Co Ltd,
  Aberdeen
Triple expansion 3-cyl
  steam reciprocating by
  North East Marine
  Engineering Co,
  Sunderland: 1,700ihp

The *James Rowan* was a large steam collier with a deadweight capacity of 3,680 tons and a speed of 11 knots. She was built as one of five sister ships for the growing CEGB fleet and launched on 26 October 1954. The others were the *Sir John Snell*, *Charles H. Merz*, *Sir William Walker* and *Sir Johnstone Wright*. They were designed for the carriage of coal from the pits on the east coast to the coal-fired power stations and other installations with discharging gear. After 29 years service she was broken up at Queenborough on 6 June 1984. This view of the *James Rowan* taken in March 1983 shows her alongside discharging coal for Shoreham power station on the Sussex coast. Her domed funnel and sloping stanchions belie the fact that she was built in the mid-1950s. For a vessel of 28 years old she was in remarkable condition when the photo was taken. *Mick Lindsay*

SIR JOHN SNELL

(8/1955) CEGB (Stephenson Clarke)
2,947grt; 340ft (103.62m) loa × 43ft 6in
    (13.25m) beam
Hall, Russell & Co Ltd, Aberdeen
Triple expansion 3-cyl steam
    reciprocating by North East Marine
    Engineering Co, Sunderland:1,700ihp

A sister ship to the *James Rowan* and her consorts, the *Sir John Snell* was designed for the same duties around the coast. By the time the five ships of this class had entered service it brought the CEGB's postwar fleet up to a strength of 30 colliers, with only two vessels having been built before the War. The *Sir John Snell* was not a flatiron collier, having a larger superstructure than the 'up-river' type of collier. Other features included the poop deck accommodation stopping short of the stern and the masts clear of the hatches. Renamed *Agmar I* she arrived at San Esteban de Pravia in Spain on 20 December 1980 for scrapping. The photograph shows the *Sir John Snell* alongside at Workington in June 1977. Then 22 years old, she looks in pristine condition with round-edged bridge structure and wooden 'monkey island'. The stumpy buff structure on her forward well deck is the hatch lifting gear. *Mick Lindsay*

KENTISH COAST

(9/1946) ex *Ulster Weaver*
(1964) ex *Jersey Coast* (1954)
ex *Ulster Duchess* (1946)
Coast Lines Ltd, Liverpool
498grt; 201ft 6in (61.41m) loa
× 30ft 2in (9.19m) beam
Ardrossan Dockyard Ltd,
Ardrossan
Oil 2SA 6-cyl by British Polar
Engines Ltd, Glasgow:
960bhp

Originally built as the *Ulster Duchess* for the Belfast Steamship Co associated with Coast Lines, the *Kentish Coast* was a general cargo open shelter deck coaster. After an eight-year stint as the *Jersey Coast* for the British Channel Islands SS Co, and a further ten years with the Belfast SS Co as the *Ulster Weaver*, she transferred to Coast Lines and entered the Liverpool–Plymouth–Southampton–London and London–Belfast routes for these owners. Although small in size she could manage around 12 knots. In 1968 she became the Kuwaiti-owned *Salmiah Coast* remaining so until deleted from Lloyd's Register in 1999. The photograph of the *Kentish Coast* was taken alongside the Victoria Wharf, adjacent to Harland & Wolff's shipyard at Belfast, in July 1967. Though registered with Coast Lines, her funnel is painted in the red and black livery of the Belfast Steamship Co. Moored abreast of her inboard is another Coast Lines vessel, the 1958-built *Cambrian Coast*. Although similar to the *Kentish Coast*, this vessel was longer but 2 knots slower. She is sporting the familiar Coast Lines funnel markings. Of interest to the extreme right of the picture is the gantry of Harland & Wolff's No 2 slip on which the White Star liner *Olympic* was built. *Mick Lindsay*

LANCASHIRE COAST

(4/1954) ex *Trojan Prince* (1969)
ex *Lancashire Coast* (1968)
Coast Lines Ltd, Liverpool
1,283grt; 256ft (78.02m) loa × 39ft 2in
(11.94m) beam
C. Hill & Sons Ltd, Bristol
Oil 2SA 5-cyl by George Clark Ltd,
Sunderland: 1,625bhp

The *Lancashire Coast* was launched on 18 November 1953 as a sister to the Cammell Laird-built *Cheshire Coast* and was originally employed on the company's London to Liverpool service. She was designed as an open shelter deck general cargo coaster with a deadweight capacity of 1,535 tons and a speed of 12 knots. Around 1966 the *Lancashire Coast* and her sister transferred for a time within the Coast Lines group to the Belfast SS Co, later switching to Burns & Laird Lines. She was chartered to Prince Line in 1968 and renamed *Trojan Prince* but reverted to her original name the following year. The *Lancashire Coast* was converted into a cattle/car carrier, having her masts and samson posts removed. She was sold out of the company in 1980 to an Italian concern and renamed *Paolino* and may well have been modified further. She was finally broken up at Salamis, Greece, during March 1984. This photograph of the *Lancashire Coast*, also seen in Belfast SS Co funnel colours and taken in June 1969, is thought to show her alongside the Walker Naval yard at Newcastle not long after her initial conversion. *Mick Lindsay*

CARDIGANBROOK

(3/1952) Comben Longstaff &
Co, London
1,780grt; 273ft (83.20m) loa
× 38ft 2in (11.63m) beam
J. Lewis & Sons Ltd,
Aberdeen
Triple expansion 3-cyl steam
reciprocating (by builder):
900ihp

The *Cardiganbrook*, launched on 29 December 1951, was the last steamship ordered by Comben Longstaff but operated for Williamstown Shipping. She entered service in 1952 along with her diesel-powered sister ship *Cardiffbrook*. She had three hatches and a deadweight capacity of 2,268 tons. A rather peculiar feature was her pronounced clipper bow which, together with her sloping squat funnel, gave her a rather modern look for the 1950s. During January 1967 she transferred to Comben Longstaff entirely. However, the move was to an all-motorship fleet with new vessels having a single accommodation block aft. The *Cardiganbrook* was sold out of the company in March 1969, to Meatmar SA, Panama and renamed *Maria Than*. She arrived at La Spezia, Italy, on 14 March 1970 to be broken up. In this photograph, thought to date from the mid-1950s, she is seen ready to load, moored at the Harton Staiths on the River Tyne, her hatchways open ready to receive cargo. Alongside her is the 1,351 gross ton collier *Tolworth*. This latter vessel was built for the Wandsworth, Wimbledon & Epsom District Gas Co Ltd in 1930 and sold in 1958 to become a harbour pontoon at Ravenna. *Kenneth Wightman*

CORMOAT

(5/1945) William Cory & Son Ltd
2,886grt; 325ft 10in (99.30m) loa × 44ft 6in (13.56m) beam
Burntisland Shipbuilding Co, Burntisland
Triple expansion 3-cyl steam reciprocating by D. Rowan & Co,
Glasgow: ihp not known

An example of the typical steam-powered general cargo coaster with raised quarterdeck and amidships bridge structure, resembling the layout of an oil tanker, is William Cory's collier *Cormoat*, seen in the late 1950s. She was launched on 29 March 1945, entering service two months later. The smoke-deflecting cowl of her funnel suggests Admiralty influence on her wartime design. The *Cormoat* appears to be moored in mid-river, presumably awaiting to discharge, while beyond her starboard side is fleet mate *Corfoss* already berthed. Sold in 1965 to Cia Naviera SA, Piraeus, the *Cormoat* was renamed *Chrigral*, seven years later becoming the *Marianik*. She was broken up at Split, Yugoslavia, from October 1974. The 1,849 gross ton *Corfoss* was scrapped eight years earlier at Santander, Spain. *Kenneth Wightman*

PASS OF GLENCLUNNIE

(5/1963) Cory Maritime Ltd
1,416grt; 245ft 2in (74.72m) loa × 37ft 10in (11.53m) beam
Sir James Laing & Sons, Sunderland
Oil 2SA 6-cyl by Nydqvist & Holm, Tröllhattan: 1,230bhp

Bound for Grangemouth, in the Firth of Forth, where her cargo would be discharged into storage tanks, is the Cory coastal tanker *Pass of Glenclunnie* painted in Panocean Group colours. She has the typical two-island layout of the refined spirit carrier. Vessels of this type often had a trunk deck linking their poop and forecastle. There is little freeboard but this presents no dangers given that her tank tops would be perfectly watertight. The flags above her bridge are, on the left, her houseflag, in the centre, the International Code of Signals letter 'B' signifying that she is carrying a hazardous cargo, and on the right, International Code of Signals letter 'H', signifying that she has a pilot aboard. In the background, between the *Pass of Glenclunnie* and the power station is what appears to be a Soviet tug. *Mick Lindsay*

EILEAN GLAS

(2/1961) ex *Th'Eilean Glas* (1972) ex *Ceres* (1971) ex *Overysel* (1968)
R. Cunningham
374grt; 156ft (47.54m) loa × 25ft (7.62m) beam
Bodewes Gruno, Foxhol
Diesel engine: bhp not known

Bought in 1971 to replace the 1935-built *Glas Island*, the *Th'Eilean Glas*, shortened a year later to *Eilean Glas*, was named after the lighthouse on Scalpeg, in the Outer Hebrides. She was a typical 'Dutch' coaster type with two masts, one on the forecastle and the other up against the bridge front. Registered at Stornaway, her owner's base, she was photographed at Workington in June 1975. This arrangement of the derricks, leaving the well deck clear, suited the stowage of timber as a deck cargo. The purpose of the long slit-like scupper in her main deck bulwark, just above her load mark, was to rapidly clear sea water from off her main deck when fully loaded in rough seas. Despite her older style, as revealed by her wooden wheelhouse, there is a substantial array of navigational and telecommunications antennae above her bridge. The *Eilean Glas* stranded one mile south of Drogheda on 1 May 1980. Declared a constructive total loss, she was broken up. *Mick Lindsay*

BRANDON

(6/1957) W.E. Dowds
586grt; 169ft 9in (51.73m) loa × 29ft 5in (8.97m) beam
Charles Hill & Sons, Bristol
Oil 4SA 6-cyl with SR and reverse gear by Ruston & Hornsby, Lincoln: 540bhp

The engines-aft motor cargo ship *Brandon* is seen in loaded condition in Cardiff docks in May 1974. Her owners, based along the coast alongside a wharf at Newport, Gwent, specialised in the handling of fertilisers, animal feed, timber, minerals, aluminium and steel. Launched on 28 February 1957 for Osborne & Wallis Ltd, making her first sailing that June, the *Brandon* was one of three similar vessels with the *Colston* and *Salcombe*. Along with other vessels of the Osborn & Wallis fleet, they conveyed coal from Newport and Ely to the power stations at Portishead. The *Brandon* is another good example of the typical British general cargo coaster with raised quarterdeck serving up-river ports around the UK but, built as colliers serving ports with automated facilities, she and her sisters lacked their own cargo-handling equipment. The raised quarterdeck arrangement was intended to improve trim when fully loaded and it was a characteristic feature of older British coasters. By 1982, Lloyd's Register had the *Brandon* listed under the ownership of Franco British Chartering Agency, managed by Gillie & Blair of Newport. *Mick Lindsay*

HAWESWATER

(7/1968) ex *Percy Dawson* (1988) Effluents Services Ltd
1,469grt; 257ft 9in (78.54m) loa × 41ft 2in (12.55m) beam
Ferguson Bros Ltd, Port Glasgow
2 × Oil 4SA 6-cyl by Mirrlees National, Stockport: 2,319bhp

Originally built for the Northwest Water (Eastern) Division, Manchester, the sludge carrier or effluents tanker *Haweswater* is seen some twenty or more years later in the private hands of Effluents Services Ltd, Manchester. Sludge disposal vessels, conveying waste from sewage works to coastal dumping grounds, were once a common sight in river estuaries near to large centres of population, in this case Southampton. Discharge was usually by gravity through doors in the bottom of the hull. A powerful twin-screw ship, capable of 12.5 knots, she was required to complete rapid round-trip voyages often against strong tidal conditions. The propellers on this type of ship were invariably controllable pitch or housed in nozzles to give them greater manoeuvrability in the restricted or shallow waters adjacent to loading berths. Her modern, enclosed bridge is indicative of completion and entry into service in the late 1960s. The crane located aft was probably intended for handling her lifeboat. After eleven years with Effluents Services Ltd, the *Haweswater* was sold on. With her name shortened to *Water*, she was the subject of a further sale within the same year, 1999, becoming the *Olympic* in the ownership of Olympic Water Transport Shipping, Piraeus.
Mick Lindsay

BORODINO

(6/1950) Ellermans Wilson Line
3,206grt; 312 ft (95.1m) loa × 48ft 8in (14.8m)
beam
Ailsa Shipbuilding Co, Troon
Triple expansion 3-cyl steam reciprocating and LP
turbine with hydraulic coupling DR geared to single
screw (by builder): hp not known

The passenger cargo steamship *Borodino*, launched on 7 February 1950, worked routes across the North Sea, mostly from Hull and London to Copenhagen, Aarhus and Odense, and she was frequently to be seen in UK coastal waters while on these runs. She could accommodate 37 First-class passengers but her main revenue was derived from her cargoes of dairy produce for which she had a capacity of 1,955 deadweight tons. The *Borodino*'s hull was painted grey in order to indicate her priority status as a ship conveying perishable goods. She continued in service for the Wilson Line, as it was more commonly known, for seventeen years, going to the breakers yard at Bruges in July 1967 after a relatively short career. The introduction of the 6,916 gross ton *Spero* no doubt hastened her demise. Wilson's fleet had dwindled in size since the early 1960s until, in 1966, the company formed a consortium with Swedish Lloyd and Svea Line in the form of the England-Sweden Line for which the *Spero* was a constituent. *Kenneth Wightman*

TEANO

(2/1955) Ellermans Wilson Line
1,580grt; 277ft 2in (84.50m) loa × 43ft 1in
(13.10m) beam
Henry Robb & Co, Leith
Triple expansion 3-cyl steam reciprocating and LP
turbine with hydraulic coupling DR geared to
single screw by Swan Hunter & Wigham
Richardson, Newcastle: hp not known

The Ellermans Wilson Line, known as the Wilson Line until 1916, when it was taken over by Ellermans, made its early fortunes from importing iron ore from Sweden. Once a substantial company, it was said that 'Hull is Wilson's and Wilson's are Hull'. The line maintained a variety of short-sea trade routes across the North Sea and via the Baltic, as well as to Southern Europe through the Mediterranean. Its fleet of green-hulled ships, like the cargo ship *Teano* shown here in drydock at Hull, were dubbed the 'green parrots'. The *Teano* was the last steam powered vessel to be completed for her owners, all new vessels that followed her being motorships. She spent 13 years working for Wilson's before she was sold for further service with Liberian owners as the *Asione*. A year later, in 1969, she was sold again, registered under the Maldives flag for Zade Shipping Co as the *Ocean Duchess*. On 13 June 1976 she suffered a fire in her engine room while at Bahrain, where she had arrived from Colombo with a cargo of tea. The outbreak spread to her poop deck and cargo hatches amidships and by the time it was extinguished she had been seriously damaged. Beached near Sitra Anchorage in a gutted and flooded condition she was declared a constructive total loss and, following sale to Pakistani shipbreakers, she was towed to Gadani Beach in February 1977 for scrapping.
Kenneth Wightman

ESSO BRIXHAM

(11/1957) Esso Petroleum Co Ltd
828grt; 196ft 1in (59.76m) loa × 34ft 5in (10.49m) beam
Philip & Son Ltd, Dartmouth
Oil 4SA 8-cyl with flexible coupling and SR reverse
gearing by English Electric Co, Preston: 1,000bhp

A typical small coastal gasoline tanker of the Esso Petroleum fleet, the *Esso Brixham* heads out to sea on a misty, winter's morning in 1972. The derrick on her foremast was used to assist in handling the hoses and pipe connections when loading and discharging fuel. Other vessels of her type and size were the sister vessels *Esso Hythe*, *Esso Lyndhurst* and *Esso Woolston*, each having a capacity of around 1,000 tons deadweight. The *Esso Brixham* was broken up at Middlesbrough from May 1980, her name shortened to *Brixham* for the delivery voyage to the scrapyard. *Mick Lindsay*

ESSO HYTHE

(5/1959) Esso Petroleum Co Ltd, London
856grt; 209ft (63.70m) loa × 35ft 3in (10.75m) beam
Henry Scarr Ltd, Hessle
Oil 4SA 8-cyl with flexible coupling and SR reverse gearing by English Electric Co, Preston: 1,000bhp

Fleet mate of the *Esso Brixham*, the coastal tanker *Esso Hythe*, passes Calshot Spit as she heads out into the Solent, fully loaded from Fawley Oil Refinery. Note the lack of freeboard when in a fully loaded condition. The *Esso Hythe* and her sisters were capable of a speed of 10 knots. Now a sport and activity centre, Calshot Spit served as a Naval Air Station from March 1913, later becoming RAF Calshot until its closure in April 1961. In the background is the Fawley power station on the edge of the New Forest. Sold in 1981, the *Esso Hythe* became the *Rim*, owned and operated by Abdullah Gandour of Tripoli. *Mick Lindsay*

ARIDITY

(7/1931) F.T. Everard & Sons
336grt; 130ft (39.62m) loa × 24ft 7in (7.49m) beam
Fellows & Co Ltd, Yarmouth
Oil 2SA 6-cyl by Newbury Diesel Co Ltd, Newbury: ca. 500bhp

After being sunk by a mine in the Thames Estuary on 19 October 1940, the *Aridity* was salved but declared a constructive total loss. Nevertheless, she was repaired and a new engine replaced her original Plenty-Still 2SA 5-cylinder plant. A prewar Everard-owned, three-island general cargo ship, she is deceiving in that, despite her age, she looks more like a steamship than a motorship. Her holds, on either side of the bridge structure, were each served by a single, long-sparred derrick. The *Aridity* is seen in June 1964 in the River Colne, near Wivenhoe, up-river from Colchester, Essex, lying at anchor as confirmed by the single black ball suspended from her forward rigging. The wisp of smoke from the galley stovepipe suggests an imminent meal break. Her 35-year career with Everards ended in July 1966 when she was sold to Greek owners and renamed *Soula*. Ten years later she was renamed again, becoming the *Star 1* following sale to Yellow Sea Marine Co, Limassol, Cyprus. In 1988, when she had reached the grand old age of 57, the former *Aridity* was deleted from Lloyd's Register but this is not to say that she did not continue trading after that date. *Mick Lindsay*

CONFORMITY

(1940) ex *C.85* (1956) F.T. Everard & Sons
484grt; 171ft 6in (52.26m) loa × 28ft 3in (8.61m) beam
W.J. Yarwood & Sons Ltd, Northwick
Triple expansion 3-cyl steam reciprocating (by builder): 385ihp

A later Everard ship, this is the steam-engined coastal tanker *Conformity* which started life as the Admiralty coaling lighter *C.85*. Beyond her, as she passes inbound on the Thames in April 1961, can be seen a number of Thames' ship-handling tugs moored near the Royal Terrace Pier, Gravesend. The distinctive feature of the *Conformity* is her saddle bridge, supported by struts extending down to the main deck, an arrangement that allowed clear movement fore and aft along the entire length of the ship. She was converted into a tanker in 1959, in the course of which she was lengthened and widened, and her tonnage increased by 140 gross tons. The *Conformity* was sold in October 1970 for breaking up at Hendrik-Ido-Ambacht, although scrapping did not, in fact, commence until late in 1973. Though not the best quality picture, this post-conversion view has been included here to show this novel vessel whose unusual configuration no doubt owes much to her genesis as an Admiralty-conceived craft. *Mick Lindsay*

SENIORITY

(12/1951) F.T. Everard & Sons
1,566grt; 242ft 6in (73.90m) loa × 38ft 2in (11.63m) beam
Goole Shipbuilding & Repairing Co Ltd, Goole
Oil 2SA 4-cyl by John I. Thornycroft, Southampton: 800bhp

ATOMICITY

(12/1947) F.T. Everard & Sons
592grt; 183ft 7in (55.95m) loa × 27ft 7in (8.41m) beam
Grangemouth Dockyard Co Ltd, Grangemouth
Oil 2SA 5-cyl by Newbury Diesel Co Ltd, Newbury: bhp not known

This view of two Everard engines-aft, general cargo ships brings us forward in time, depicting the postwar-built pair *Seniority* and *Atomicity*, believed to be moored off Greenhithe. The *Seniority* was one of what were commonly referred to as 'yellow perils', sporting the yellow hull and funnel colouring adopted by Everard's grain-carrying vessels. Both the *Seniority* and *Atomicity* were motorships, reflecting the change to propulsive power that became commonplace after the Second World War. Both ships found employment under the Greek flag in the closing years of their careers, after sale out of the Everard fleet. The *Atomicity* was sold in March 1966 and renamed *Eolos*, only to be mined off Tripoli, Libya on 21 June 1973 while en route from Kavalla, Macedonia, to Tripoli with a cargo of limestone. The mine was one of a quantity laid by the Libyan authorities to deter Israeli sabotage units but which had floated free. The *Seniority* became the *Salefterios* in 1971, under the Cypriot flag, prior to being broken up at Aviles, North Spain from May 1972. *Kenneth Wightman*

29

CLARITY

(3/1957) F.T. Everard & Sons Ltd
763grt; 204ft (62.17m) loa × 30ft 3in (9.22m) beam
Goole Shipbuilding & Repairing Co Ltd, Goole
Oil 2SA 6-cyl by Newbury Diesel Co Ltd, Newbury: 600bhp

High and dry on a mud berth at Greenhithe with other coasting craft, is the *Clarity*, her flat bottom permitting her to safely beach at low tide without risk of capsizing (see also the *Glenshira* on page 40). The *Clarity*'s bilge keels are also evident, a feature which aided stability in a seaway and gave the hull increased strength. Launched on 12 April 1956, she did not enter service until almost a year later. From November 1971 she transferred to Everard Shipping Co ownership. Two years earlier she had been re-engined with a comparable sized engine. Note how, for some unknown reason, the *Clarity*'s red boot-topping does not extend right aft. In February 1978 the *Clarity* was sold to Panamanian owners Olympios Shipping Ltd and renamed *Agios Thomas*. She was broken up at Augusta, Sicily in 1984. *Mick Lindsay*

WILLIAM J. EVERARD

(3/1963) Everard Shipping Co Ltd
1,589grt; 265ft 9in (81.01m) loa × 39ft 3in (11.97m) beam
Goole Shipbuilding & Repairing Co Ltd, Goole
Vee-Oil 4SA 8-cyl by British Polar Engines Ltd, Glasgow: 1,540bhp

Everard's, which was probably the largest and best-known fleet of British coasters, finally lost its independent identity in 2007, purchased by and absorbed into the company of James Fisher & Sons, examples of whose coasters may also be seen on the pages that immediately follow. Back in 1963, when the *William J. Everard* entered service, her owners remained very much a family concern. She is seen berthed at Avonmouth with her MacGregor hatch covers on the forward hold fully retracted for working cargo. The dust emerging from the hold, also the lorry on the quayside with its trailer fully raised, suggests that loading is well under way. Her rust-streaked and scraped hull, typifying the wear and tear routinely inflicted upon hard-working coasters, is in need of a fresh coat of paint. Note the electric motors, sited on the tabernacle at the base of each mast, which drove the winches that operated her derricks. The *William J. Everard* was re-engined in May 1974, her original two-stroke 8-cylinder diesel, supplied by Nydqvist & Holm A/B of Tröllhattan and rated at 1,000 brake horsepower, replaced by a more powerful British Polar unit. She had a rather chequered career after she was sold out of the Everard fleet in January 1982. She was acquired by Wimpey Marine, London, which had her converted into a drillship named *Wimpey Geocore*. Her owners became Wimpey Laboratories from 1984. Four years later she was sold to Olympia Shipping Ltd, Gibraltar and rebuilt as a dry cargo vessel with the name *Seaburn Girl*. Resold again, in 1990, she passed to Leighton Shipping Ltd, Gibraltar, renamed *Husum*. *Mick Lindsay*

POOL FISHER

(9/1959) James Fisher & Sons Ltd
1,028grt; 217ft 6in (66.28m) loa × 33ft 10in (10.31m) beam
N.V. Schpsw. 'Foxhol', Foxhol
Oil 4SA 6-cyl by Klöckner-Humboldt-Deutz, Cologne: 830bhp

Typical of the smart, modern dry cargo coasters that entered service from the late 1950s onwards, the *Pool Fisher* features a long, unencumbered cargo deck forward of her engines-aft bridge, accommodation and machinery structure. The forward hatch, in the well deck, was served by her own derricks but those serving the after hatch have been removed. The *Pool Fisher* is seen at Whitehaven, Cumbria in 1974. The large warehouse to the left on the quayside bears the discolorations of removed lettering which, nevertheless, reveal that it was once owned by Quaker Oats Limited. The *Pool Fisher* sank 8 nautical miles south of St Catherine's Light, Isle of Wight in very heavy weather on 6 November 1979. She was bound from Hamburg to Runcorn with a cargo of potash. Twelve members of her crew and the wife of her Chief Engineer were drowned. There were just two survivors. *Mick Lindsay*

MARCHON ENTERPRISE

(2/1962) Albright & Wilson Ltd
1,599grt; 261ft 2in (79.60m) loa × 39ft 3in (11.97m) beam
Clelands Shipbuilding Co Ltd, Wallsend-on-Tyne
Oil 4SA 8-cyl by Klöckner-Humboldt-Deutz, Cologne: 1,800bhp

This lovely study of a coaster on a calm, wind-less day, resulting in spectacularly clear reflections, shows the *Marchon Enterprise*, managed by James Fisher on behalf of Albright & Wilson of Whitehaven, alongside at Workington at her owners' chemical works in 1977 having discharged a cargo of phosphate rock. She had previously been with the James Fisher subsidiary, Leo Lines. Her hatch covers are open back to the bridge front but there is little sign of activity, the two shore-side cranes parked in virtually complete symmetry. The photograph may have been taken during a work break. She was broken up at Manchester from 14 June 1984.
Mick Lindsay

DERWENT FISHER

(2/1966) James Fisher & Sons Ltd
1,096grt; 216ft 11in (66.11m) loa × 34ft 2in (10.41m) beam
N.V. Nieuwe Noord Ned. Schpsw, Groningen
Oil 4SA 8-cyl by Klöckner-Humboldt-Deutz, Cologne:
  1,060bhp

Compared with her previously-illustrated fleet mate, the *Derwent Fisher*, photographed at Workington in 1975, is in a smart and clean condition. Her MacGregor hatches are drawn back and the cargo is being unloaded by a shore-side mobile crane onto a waiting truck. Other trucks wait their turn to come alongside to receive their load of what appear to be pre-cast concrete blocks. The *Derwent Fisher* was renamed no less than seven times from 1979, after she was sold by James Fisher: *Parham* (1979), *Sofia* (1984), *Saint Anthonys* (1989), *Golduen Bird* (1990), *Mariya* (1991), *Swene* (1996) and *Baris B.* (1996). She was finally broken up in Turkey in April 2002.
Mick Lindsay

SANDPIPER

(6/1957) General Steam Navigation Co (GSNCo)
916grt; 232ft 6in (70.87m) loa × 37ft 7in (11.46m) beam
H. Robb, Leith
Oil 2SA 8-cyl by British Polar Engines, Glasgow: bhp not known

The *Sandpiper*, a near-sister to the *Gannet* and *Heron,* was launched on 1 May 1957. Her design typified the route she was meant to serve. An open shelter deck type with some refrigerated capacity, she was constructed with continuous bulwarks, a solid base to the superstructure and a mainmast forward of the third hatch. Although primarily designed to operate between London and continental ports, she was capable of service to North America as many GSNCo ships operated between the St Lawrence and Hudson Bay in the summer months. In 1967 she was sold to French buyers and renamed *Ile de Saint Pierre*. She was sold again in 1981 and became the *Alinda*, then the *Katia K* in 1981. She was finally renamed *Voyager II* for her journey to the breakers at Gadani Beach, Pakistan, where she arrived on 18 April 1989 for demolition. In the undated photograph she is seen in well-maintained condition in the West India Docks, London. *Kenneth Wightman*

DRYBURGH

(10/1952) Anchor Gas Tankers Ltd
(George Gibson & Co Ltd)
1,593grt; 260ft 7in (79.41m) loa × 38ft 1in (11.61m)
beam
Grangemouth Dockyard Co Ltd, Grangemouth
Oil 2SA 8-cyl by British Polar Engines, Glasgow:
1,520bhp

The Liquefied Gas Carrier *Dryburgh*, from a view taken in April 1979 at Eastham Locks, was originally completed as a general cargo ship working her owners' short-sea routes between Aberdeen, Grangemouth and Dundee and continental ports as far afield as The Netherlands and Portugal. She was converted into a tanker in 1962, a modification that increased her gross tonnage by almost 50 per cent and her deadweight capacity to 1,380 tons. She is flying the International Code of Signals red 'Bravo' flag signifying that her cargo is dangerous or hazardous. Alongside it is her houseflag. Virtually hove to and making slow progress, she is waiting to enter the locks at the entrance to the Manchester Ship Canal with Garston Docks in the distance to the right. Her funnel colours are those of the Unigas pool. The *Dryburgh* continued in service until February 1985 when she was broken up at Gadani Beach, Pakistan. *Mick Lindsay*

ARRAN FIRTH

(11/1957) ex *Alfa* (1962)
G.T. Gillie & Blair (Firth Shipping Co Ltd)
544grt; 188ft 7in (57.48m) loa × 28ft 3in (8.61m) beam
Grol's Scheepswerken, Zuidbroek
Oil 4SA 6-cyl by Masch. Kiel AG, Kiel: 480bhp

This May 1969 photograph shows a typical so-called 'Dutch' type coaster, the *Arran Firth*, completed twelve years earlier as the *Alfa* for I/S Alfa, Copenhagen, which passed into the ownership of the Newcastle-based concern of Gillie & Blair five years later. She was acquired to replace the *Beauly Firth* and augment Gillie & Blair's existing three-ship fleet comprising the *Moray Firth IV*, *Olna Firth* and *Pentland Firth*. By 1972 the *Arran Firth* had been sold along with two of her fleet mates, the *Moray Firth IV*. Unlike other similar ships of the time, she retains an old-style cylindrical funnel. Her long derricks are in the stowed position, supported amidships by a combined ventilator cross-stay. *Mick Lindsay*

SHIELDHALL

(10/1955) Glasgow Corporation
1,792grt; 268ft (81.69m) loa × 44ft 7in (13.59m) beam
Lobnitz & Co Ltd, Renfrew
Triple expansion 6-cyl steam reciprocating (by builder): 1,600ihp

Laid down in 1954 for the Glasgow Corporation, the effluent vessel *Shieldhall* could transport 1,840 tons of treated sewage sludge down the River Clyde from Glasgow to be dumped out at sea. She also had the facilities to carry 80 day passengers when operating during the summer months. In 1977 she was sold to Southern Water to carry sludge from Woolston, near Southampton, to waters south of the Isle of Wight. Withdrawn from service in 1985, she was purchased in 1988 for the sum of £20,000 by Southampton City's Museums who planned to preserve her. She now operates excursions and charters for the Solent Steam Packet Ltd and is manned and maintained by a workforce of volunteers. Her income from day cruises is supplemented by occasional engagements to serve as a period film setting. The photograph taken in August 1963 shows the *Shieldhall* on the River Clyde near Gourock. Although a postwar vessel, she has a traditional wheelhouse, is of riveted and welded construction, with a straight stem and cruiser stern. Of interest in the background, beyond the *Shieldhall*'s well deck, may be seen the paddle steamer *Waverley* heading in the direction of Dunoon. *Mick Lindsay*

PIBROCH

(7/1957) Glenlight Shipping Co Ltd
157grt; 87ft 5in (26.65m) loa × 20ft 6in (6.23m) beam
Scott & Sons, Bowling
Oil 2SA 5-cyl by British Polar Engines, Glasgow: 270bhp

The motor coaster *Pibroch* follows the general layout of the original Clyde steam puffers having bluff bows, a single large hold and a single mast with derrick mounted on the forecastle. In older puffers, the crew's quarters with cooking stove were located in the forepeak while the skipper had a small cabin in the stern. However, in later built vessels like the *Pibroch*, all accommodation was placed under the poop deck. The wheelhouse and funnel stood directly above the engine room. These craft had a flat bottom, allowing them to beach at low tide at ports of call which did not have piers (see the *Glenshira* on page 40). Puffer craft – now a generic term embracing both steam and motor-driven vessels – provided a vital supply service to the west coast of Scotland and islands of the Hebrides, a service maintained until 1993 by Glenlight Shipping Co, Greenock, which had acquired the *Pibroch* from Scottish Malt Distillers in 1975. Glenlight sold her to J.A. Hawco, Glasgow in 1990 and thereafter she moved to Ireland where she languished for many years until abandoned at Letterfrack, Connemara. The *Pibroch* is high and dry, photographed on a slipway at an unknown location in March 1976, no doubt undergoing a routine overhaul. *Mick Lindsay*

TYRRONALL

(1935) ex *Empire Contamar* (1948) ex *Heimat* (1945)
A.J. Gough
248grt; 136ft (41.45m) loa × 23ft (7.01m) beam
Flender, Lubeck-Siems
Oil engine: bhp not known

Another little coaster with a very chequered history, the *Tyrronall* started life as the three-masted schooner *Heimat* for H. Rubarth of Hamburg, launched on 18 July 1935. In 1945, during the closing stages of the Second World War, she was seized by the Allies at Kiel and commandeered by the Ministry of War Transport as the *Empire Contamar*. In 1947 she was wrecked on a reef in St Austell Bay but later that year she was raised and rebuilt as the *Tyrronall* for F. J. Tyrrell of Cardiff. In 1961 she transferred her ownership to James Tyrrell of Arklow. After seven years with them, she was sold for further trading to A. J. Gough of Essex. She was finally scrapped at Santander in Spain in 1974. The *Tyrronall* is seen photographed at Newport, Isle of Wight, in June 1974. This was the River Medina's head of navigation and by the look of it the falling tide will have left her high and dry on the mud alongside the quay. Notice the unusually large grilled scuppers in her gunwales for the shedding of water in heavy seas. The Jacob's ladder over her side would have been used for hull inspection at low tide. *Ray Sprake*

GRAYBANK

(3/1957) ex *Hillswick* (1968) ex *Greta* (1964) G.E. Gray & Sons
382grt; 156ft 6in (47.70m) loa × 26ft 6in (8.10m) beam
Scheepsw 'Kerstholt', Groningen
Oil 4SA 6-cyl by Masch Kiel AG, Kiel: 360bhp

This vessel was originally built as the typical Dutch coaster *Greta* for J. Schokkenbroek of Groningen and launched on 22 December 1956. She and many of her type of between 200 to 500gross ton were pioneers in the short-sea coastal trade. In 1964 she was bought by Enid Shipping Co Ltd of Leith and renamed *Hillswick* and later sold on to G.E. Gray & Sons of Chatham as the *Graybank*. After seven years with Gray's she was sold again in 1975 and renamed *Judert II*. On 9 November 1976, while off the Suffolk coast, east of Felixstowe, bound for the approaches to the Thames estuary, she was in collision in position 52°05'N, 2°11'E. It is not known whether she was sunk in this accident. The photograph shows a well-maintained *Graybank* alongside, possibly at Whitehaven, in June 1971. *Mick Lindsay*

JOHN PERRING

(4/1926)
Greater London Council
(GLC)/London County Council (LCC)
1,653grt; 267ft (81.38m) loa × 43ft
8in (13.31m) beam
W. Beardmore, Dalmuir
Triple expansion 6-cyl steam
reciprocating (by builder): ihp not
known

The *John Perring* was launched on 26 February 1926 and completed less than two months later as an effluent tanker for the then London County Council. She was one of the original sludge carriers designed to transport sewage from the digested sludge pump house adjacent to the Beckton water treatment (sewage) works down the river for discharge in the Thames estuary. She was joined by other sludge carriers, namely the *Edward Cruse* in 1954 and the motorship *Bexley* in 1966. Her ownership changed when the LCC begat the GLC, although her duties remained the same. In 1968 two more motor-driven tankers joined the GLC fleet, the *Hounslow* and *Newham*, making the aged *John Perring* surplus to requirements. She arrived at Inverkeithing for scrapping on 1 June 1968. This photograph shows the *John Perring* alongside at an unidentified location in September 1964. Her 1920s lines are clear to see but, despite being 38 years old, she appears to be well maintained. She has the number '51' below the bridge and the Council's armorial shield in full colour on her funnel. *Kenneth Wightman*

(5/1924) ex *Dan C. Kingman* (1962) ex *Sandon 3* (1957)
ex *Dan C. Kingman* (1954) Hall & Co
2,437grt; 253ft 11in (77.39m) loa × 46ft 4in (14.12m) beam
Sun Shipbuilding & Drydock Co, Chester, Pennsylvania
2 × Oil 4SA 12-cyl by Mirrlees National: bhp not known

The *A.A. Raymond* was originally launched as the *Dan C. Kingman* on 22 March 1924. As such she was one of the large twin-screw dredgers then operated by the United States Army Engineer Corps. She was built possibly as a steamer with two tall funnels spaced well apart, and was in much demand as a suction dredger. Another original feature was a lightship-type beacon amidships to alert shipping during dredging operations. From 1954 to 1957 she became the *Sandon 3* before reinstating her original name. In 1962 she was purchased by Hall & Co and crossed to the UK where it is believed that she may have been re-engined with second-hand Mirrlees National diesel engines in 1963. Her demolition commenced on 7 July 1971 at Bilbao in Spain. This photograph, taken during October 1966, shows her counter stern and straight stem as features from a bygone era. Note that the two original tall funnels have been replaced by a small motorship-style one. *Kenneth Wightman*

GLENSHIRA

(1/1953) Hay Hamilton Ltd (Glenlight Shipping Ltd)
153grt; 86ft 6in (26.36m) loa × 20ft 3in (6.18m) beam
Scott & Sons, Bowling
Oil 2SA 5-cyl by British Polar Engines, Glasgow: bhp not known

The *Glenshira* was a pioneering diesel-powered version of the Clyde 'puffer' built to the dimensions of the Crinan Canal, known as an 'outside boat'. She is seen beached at an unknown location in 1976. From the River Clyde and its estuary ports, craft like the *Glenshira* loaded anthracite, coal and other vital cargoes destined to island inhabitants and to Scottish west coast ports. They then sailed via the Clyde Estuary to Loch Fyne, through the Crinan Canal to the islands of Jura and Colonsay, or continuing on to other ports such as Tarbert and Stornoway. The trade continued until 1993 when, on the withdrawal of Government subsidies, the Glenlight Shipping of Greenock suspended operations. Thereafter, road links, where bridges existed, and vehicular transport on roll-on–roll-off ferries took over. The *Glenshira* is shown prior to major modifications in 1982, after she had transferred to Ferry Services & Supplies Ltd, Glasgow. These involved the replacement of her original engine with a 2-stroke single-acting 3-cylinder plant delivering 150bhp supplied by National Gas & Oil Engine Co, Ashton-under-Lyne. At the same time her stem was fitted with bow sheaves for salvage work. She was sold for scrapping at Holyhead in March 2004.
Ray Sprake

This vessel's history is somewhat scant and it is open to speculation as to whether this Customs' steam launch was in fact built by Henry Scarr of Hessle or Richard Dunston of Thorne. This may be purely academic as Richard Dunston took over the shipyard of Henry Scarr at Hessle in 1932 when boat-building at Thorne ceased to be viable. A clue may be her Scarr's Yard No. 384. The *Dolphin* was the last steam launch built for the HM Customs for, with effect from 1937, all of the organisation's future large launches were powered by diesel engines. She was based at Gravesend to serve the River Thames area and survived the war to be sold by HM Customs in 1963. In this view of the *Dolphin* she is seen passing Tilbury Landing Stage heading down-river on her way to the Customs' depot at Gravesend. Although the photo is undated it is thought it may be from around 1960/61. In the background are Tilbury-Gravesend ferries, passenger-type on the left, car-carrier to the right. *Kenneth Wightman*

DOLPHIN

(1936)
HM Customs & Excise
118 grt; 65ft (19.81m) loa
× 17ft 6in (5.33m) beam
Henry Scarr, Hessle
Steam reciprocating
engine: 281ihp

41

JAMES JACKSON GRUNDY

(7/1948) Imperial Chemical Industries (ICI)
201grt; 102ft 9in (31.32m) loa × 22ft 1in (6.73m) beam
W. J. Yarwood & Sons, Northwich
Oil 2SA 4-cyl by Crossley Bros, Manchester: bhp not known

Launched on 30 October 1947, the *James Jackson Grundy* was one of a trio of barges to enter service in 1948 with the Nobel Division of ICI to carry the company's products for transhipment at Liverpool Docks. Her sisters, the *Comberbach* and the *Cuddington*, were placed with the Mond Division, to which the *James Jackson Grundy* was later transferred. By 1972 ICI had disposed of all their steam-driven vessels and had a fleet of ten motorships. In this photo of the *James Jackson Grundy*, taken in June 1966, she is seen off Eastham on the River Mersey inward bound for the ICI depot at Northwich on the River Weaver. At nearly 30 years old her owners have kept her in a remarkable condition. After a period as a Sea Cadet training vessel, the *James Jackson Grundy*, having reverted to her original name, has been restored for preservation. *Mick Lindsay*

Island Transport Co Ltd motor barges, fitted with Kelvin diesels:

SHALFLEET
(1962)
96ft 5in (29.39m)
J. Samuel White & Co, Cowes

CALBOURNE
(1952)
90ft 9in (27.66m)
J. Samuel White & Co, Cowes

ARRETON
(1916)
98ft 2in (29.92m)
Dobsons, Newcastle

Under the shadow of the large hammer-head crane in the J. Samuel White shipyard at Cowes are the three small motor barges *Shalfleet*, *Calbourne* and *Arreton*, photographed in the year in which they were transferred to the ownership of Vectis Shipping, a Red Funnel Group subsidiary. Motor barges such as these, which transported commercial goods to the Isle of Wight up to the late 1970s, were as distinctive at that end of the UK as the Clyde 'puffer' trade to the Western Isles was at the other. There were three principal companies engaged in this business: Island Transport Co, Vectis Shipping and, after the Second World War, British Road Services, all operating comparable single-hold vessels of around 100 gross tons and 95 feet (28.95m) overall length. Some, like the *Calbourne*, shown here, and the *Needles* (see page 9) had a large mast mounted up forward. The Island Transport Company, formed in 1923 by J. Samuel White & Co, ceased trading in 1974 and its three vessels, the only motor barges it had owned, were sold to rival Vectis Shipping. Two had been built by the parent company while the *Arreton*, a former First World War X-craft, was acquired in 1922 prior to the formation of the Island Transport subsidiary. Note her unusual truncated maierform bow. After her cross-Solent employment ended the *Arreton* transferred to Hayle, north Cornwall. It has been suggested that she is now a hulk on the River Avon, housing chickens! The *Shalfleet* became the *Spurn Bank*, trading on the north-east coast, while the *Calbourne* remains to this day on the River Medina, laid up inactive at Newport. *Mick Lindsay*

ILE DE SERK

(1941) ex *Island Commodore* (1969) ex *Channel Coast* (1950)
Isle of Sark Shipping
195grt; 98ft 5in (30.00m) loa × 20ft 11in (6.38m) beam
Rowhedge Iron Works Co, Rowhedge
Oil 2SA 6-cyl by H. Widdip & Co, Keighley: 360bhp

The *Ile de Serk* started life as the wartime-built *Channel Coast* but by 1950 had been bought by Commodore Shipping of Guernsey and renamed *Island Commodore*. Although primarily a cargo coaster she was licensed to carry 144 passengers between St Peter Port and the Isle of Sark, three times a week. When the Isle of Sark Shipping was set up in 1969, it purchased her as a going concern to maintain Sark's passenger and cargo services, and she was then renamed *Ile de Serk*. As visitors to Sark and Herm grew to some 55,000 per year, the purpose-built *Bon Marin de Serk* was introduced in 1983 to replace her on this route. This clear photograph, taken in June 1981, shows the 40 year old *Ile de Serk* in calm waters as she approaches St Peter Port. A small group of passengers may be seen on her well deck, also on the monkey island. She is in peak condition given that she had only two years left in service! *Mick Lindsay*

HOOTERN

(1/1958) ex *Dolphin City* (1974) ex *Dolphin G* (1973) ex *Martinistad* (1971)
R. Lapthorn & Co Ltd
490grt; 173ft 11in (53.00m) loa × 27ft 11in (8.50m) beam
Bijolt, Foxhol
Oil 4SA 6-cyl by Klöckner-Humboldt-Deutz, Cologne: 400bhp

The *Hootern* was originally launched on 21 September 1957 for the Dutch coaster company Scheepvaartbedrijt Martinistad of Dordrecht, as the *Martinistad*. She had a deadweight capacity of 688 tons. In 1971 she was renamed *Dolphin G*, two years later becoming the *Dolphin City* for City of London Tankers Ltd. Sold on to Lapthorn's in 1974, she became the *Hootern*. Another change of ownership followed in 1977 when she was renamed *River Taw*. Further trading in the Caribbean ensued until she was stranded off St Kitts on 8 September 1981, later towed to Martinique to become a hulk. The *Hootern* is seen in this view alongside at Camber Dock, Old Portsmouth, unloading coal during July 1976. Her sleek, continental lines and pristine paintwork belie the fact that she was some 18 years old when the photo was taken. *Mick Lindsay*

JEAN INGELOW

(3/1950) Lincoln & Hull Marine Contractors Ltd
149grt; 104ft 5in (31.83m) loa × 25ft 1in (7.65m) beam
H. Robb, Leith
Oil 4SA 6-cyl with SR gearing by Ruston & Hornsby,
Lincoln: 204bhp

The *Jean Ingelow* was launched on 7 March 1950 and completed in the same month. She was originally ordered for the Port of Boston Authority as a grab hopper dredger to dredge Boston harbour after the War when the port was seeking to expand commercially. By the mid-1970s the dredging operation was hived off to private contractors and the *Jean Ingelow* transferred to Lincoln & Hull Marine Contractors. This concern's sphere of operations included other East Anglian ports such as Kings Lynn and Great Yarmouth as well as others further up the east coast as far as Hull. The photograph shows the *Jean Ingelow* leaving Great Yarmouth in July 1983, well loaded with river mud. Her grab crane is stowed on the open hatchway. *Mick Lindsay*

INSISTENCE

(4/1939) ex *Goldgnome*
  (1952) ex *Empire Tulip*
  (1947) ex *Pallas* (1940)
London & Rochester
  Trading Co Ltd, London
290grt; 131ft 2in (39.98m)
  loa × 23ft 8in (7.21m)
  beam
Schps. Delfzijl v/h Sander
Oil 4SA 6-cyl by Bergius
  Kelvin Co, Glasgow:
  300bhp

A vessel with a chequered career, the *Insistence* was launched as a Dutch coaster, the *Pallas*, on 9 March 1939 for N. Engelsman of Delfzijl and she completed five months service before the Second World War broke out. In 1940 she was in the UK at the time when the Germans occupied The Netherlands and she was commandeered by the Ministry of War Transport which renamed her *Empire Tulip*. In 1947 she was sold to E.J. & W. Goldsmith of London and became the *Goldgnome*. Later, she was purchased by London & Rochester in 1951 and renamed *Insistence*. After an almost 20-year career with them she was broken up in Rochester from 12 December 1970. This undated view shows the *Insistence* approaching the West Pier at Gravesend, her hatches open in readiness to work cargo. Just beyond her may be seen the Tilbury–Gravesend passenger ferry alongside the terminal.
Kenneth Wightman

LIBATION

(1969) Crescent Shipping
(London & Rochester
Trading)
198grt; 100ft 6in (30.64m)
loa × 22ft 8in (6.91m)
beam
London & Rochester
Trading Co, Stroud
Oil 6-cyl by English
Electric Diesels Ltd,
Kelvin Marine Division,
Glasgow: 240bhp

Alongside at Bryants Wharf, South Quay, Great Yarmouth is the tiny coaster *Libation*, a small vessel built at the yard of her operator's parent company. The grain silos in the background suggest the nature of the cargo which she would, no doubt, be shortly loading. When fully loaded there would have been virtually no freeboard at the main deck level, as revealed by the position of her load mark. Lacking cargo-handling gear of her own, she depended on shore-side cranes or other loading and discharge facilities. The *Libation*'s near vertical sides would have facilitated cargo stowage and trim, a matter of vital consideration affecting the safety of small coasters that were constantly at risk of cargo movement. She has rubbing and strengthening strakes running along either side of her hull, the former an essential requisite to reduce the wear and tear on the hull from frequent berthing manoeuvres. A crew member touches up the paintwork on her railings between voyages. *Mick Lindsay*

SALVOR

(10/1947) Mersey Docks & Harbour Board
(MDHB), Liverpool
671grt; 173ft 6in (53.8m) loa × 35ft 6in (10.82m) beam
Ferguson Bros Ltd, Port Glasgow
Triple expansion 6-cyl steam reciprocating
(by builder): 1,300ihp

In order to maintain the busy waters of the River Mersey and Liverpool Docks complex, the MDHB operated its own small fleet of pilot tenders, salvage ships and buoy tenders. These took over the estuarial work of the River Mersey where the remit of Trinity House left off. One such vessel was the salvage ship *Salvor*, launched on the Clyde on 24 April 1947. It should be remembered that in an era before radar when there were fogs on the outer reaches of the Mersey, collision was a strong possibility in what was then a busy seaway. The *Salvor* had two substantial masts, rigged with heavy lift derricks, as well as bow sheaves. She was also equipped with high pressure fire-fighting nozzles mounted on the masts' crosstrees. All in all she was a utility vessel, later augmented by the 728 gross ton *Vigilant* completed in 1953. After 31 years with the MDHB the *Salvor* was broken up at Garston from 29 November 1978. The photograph, taken from high up on an adjacent vessel, shows the *Salvor* alongside at Liverpool during June 1970. The fire hose nozzles are clearly seen on the mainmast crosstree and on the tabernacle below. This view also reveals the detail of the spark-arresting cowl fitted atop her funnel. A member of the crew can be seen seated beneath the after conning wheel, probably enjoying his 'smoko'. *Kenneth Wightman*

THOMAS M

(6/1938) ex *Ngakoa*
  (1946) Metcalf Motor
  Coasters
593grt; 192ft 8in (58.70m)
  loa × 27ft 3in (8.30m)
  beam
De Groot & v. Vliet,
  Slikkerveer
Oil 4SA 8-cyl with SR
  gearing by Lister
  Blackstone Marine Ltd,
  Dursley: 480bhp

The London-registered, flush-decked general cargo coaster *Thomas M* looks very smart as she negotiates the confined space of Penzance harbour, Cornwall. She may be manoeuvring into the fuel berth which can be seen on the extreme left of the picture. Her single derrick on the mainmast is evidently used for her lifeboat but was also probably deployed moving ship's stores on board. Both her masts are hinged to permit clearance under low bridges. No doubt this is also the explanation for her squat funnel. The *Thomas M* was completed as the *Ngakoa* for W.A. Wilson, Southampton, passing into Metcalf's ownership after the Second World War. She was lengthened in 1958, increasing her cargo capacity to 759 deadweight tons. Nine years later she was sold on, having a chequered career in Mediterranean waters for the next 31 years: *Milos III* (1967), *Maria S.* (1973), *Maria Pia* (1974), *Evangelia* (1976) and *Sofia* (1977). She was deleted from Lloyd's Register in 1998. *Mick Lindsay*

ROBERT M

(1/1970) ex *Cree* (1977) Metcalf Motor Coasters
1,593grt; 279ft (85.04m) loa × 42ft (12.81m) beam
Hong Kong & Whampoa Dock Co, Hong Kong
Vee Oil 4SA 4-cyl by Masch. Augsburg Nurnburg (M.A.N.), Augsburg: 2,200bhp

Though not completed until 1970 and not in the United Kingdom's coastal trade until seven years later, this interesting three-island coastal tanker has been included here as an example of a larger vessel of her type and because she features another variant of the saddle bridge. Built in the Far East, she was acquired by Metcalf's after working seven years for the Indo-China Steam Navigation Co (Hong Kong) Ltd, a Jardine Matheson concern. In this 1980 photograph, the *Robert M* appears to be hove to in the approaches to Cardiff with Penarth Head in the background. Virtually dead in the water, it is not evident whether she is arriving or departing. She has the typical trunk deck of the coastal tanker with central catwalks connecting the poop, bridge structure and forecastle. Metcalf's disposed of her in 1997 when she was renamed *Nesa 1* before, later that same year, she was renamed again, becoming the *Nesa R* of Haswell Ltd, registered at Kingstown in St Vincent & The Grenadines, a convenience flag state. *Mick Lindsay*

VIOLET-MITCHELL

(1957) ex *Aspera* (1979) H.R. Mitchell & Sons Ltd
385grt; 157ft 8in (48.04m) loa × 26ft 2in (7.98m) beam
A. Vuijk & Zeneris Scheepswerven NV, Capelle
Oil 2SA 6-cyl by NV Mach. 'Bolnes', Krimpen: 220bhp

Another 'Dutch'-type coaster, the *Violet-Mitchell* is seen alongside a wharf on the River Nene at Wisbech, Cambridgeshire, 10 miles from the river's mouth on The Wash. A shore-side mobile crane handles sacks of cargo being loaded into or discharged from her forward hold. The picture exemplifies the function of the small general cargo coaster, taking a variety of essential cargoes to up-river ports around the UK. Cargoes commonly shipped through Wisbech were bricks, timber and fertilizers. Launched on 20 August 1957, the *Violet-Mitchell* spent 22 years with her original owners, J. Pronk of Groningen, prior to acquisition for the British coastal trade. *Mick Lindsay*

ORION

(1938) Hermann Muller, Hamburg
239grt; 132ft 1in (40.26m) loa × 23ft 1in (7.04m) beam
Werft Nobiskrug, Rendsburg
Oil 4SA 4-cyl by Deutsche Werke AG, Kiel: 200bhp

The small German coaster *Orion* is pictured berthed at Southampton's Town Quay in August 1967, providing a vivid reminder of how this port area used to look prior to the extensive redevelopment that has taken place there over the years since. She is heavily laden with a cargo of timber, supported in place above her main deck by vertical wooden stays inserted between the bulwarks and the horizontal timber lengths. Note how her centrally-placed mast with its twin derricks is isolated amidst the cargo and is effectively redundant as far as the unloading of this cargo is concerned. For a vessel of her age she is in exceptional condition and her modern-style funnel belies her origins, back in the late 1930s. Her general appearance suggests the possibility of modernisation having taken place at some time during the interim. She was managed for Hermann Muller by Johs. Thode, a company with offices in the same German port which had a sizeable coasting fleet of its own. *David Williams*

EBBW

(3/1948) J. Murphy & Sons
823grt; 184ft 4in (56.18m) loa × 34ft 1in (10.39m) beam
C. Hill & Sons, Bristol
Triple expansion steam reciprocating by Plenty & Son Ltd, Newbury: ihp not known

The steam hopper barge *Ebbw*, seen at Cardiff, was completed for the British Transport Docks Board (BTDB) to work in conjunction with dredging craft that either had no silt or spoil hopper spaces of their own or which, for greater efficiency, remained on station undisturbed continuing with their dredging activities while spoil was removed for them. In 1971, after 23 years service with BTDB, the *Ebbw* was sold to the local concern of J. Murphy, in whose colours she is shown here. Her hopper space appears to be divided centrally by a longitudinal bulkhead with its outer walls lower along the sides of the hull, possibly to expedite discharge. Two years later J. Murphy, in turn, sold her on to another Cardiff company, J. Carney & Sons. A year later she was deleted from Lloyd's Register and the *Ebbw*'s ultimate fate is not known by the authors. *Kenneth Wightman*

HELMSDALE

(5/1956) Northern Shipping & Trading Co (J.C. Simpson), Aberdeen
402grt; 153ft 5in (46.76m) loa × 26ft 5in (8.05m) beam
Jos. L. Meyer, Papenburg
Oil 4SA 6-cyl by Klöckner-Humboldt-Deutz, Cologne: 500bhp

Conveying in a single picture the domain of the coaster, the *Helmsdale* is seen passing close to the Scottish coast in 1972, bound for the Northern Isles. She has distinctive derrick stowage cross-stays amidships, between her holds, which serve as combined hold ventilators (see also the *Violet-Mitchell* on page 51 which has a similar structure but which is jointed centrally into a single vent). The *Helmsdale* does not have the usual lines of the raised quarterdeck coaster, having plated bulwarks for a short distance alongside her bridge structure. Likewise, her vertical stanchions reflect an older design. Unlike most coasters of her size, she carries two lifeboats which may suggest that she was certificated to carry a small number of passengers on a route that was not served regularly by ferry, although this cannot be confirmed. Stranded on 7 December 1980, the *Helmsdale* was assessed as not being worth the cost of repairs so, instead, she was broken up. *Mick Lindsay*

MR THERM

(5/1936) North Thames
  Gas Board
2,974grt; 329ft (100.27m)
  loa × 45ft 8in (13.91m)
  beam
S.P. Austin & Son,
  Sunderland
Triple expansion 3-cyl
  steam reciprocating by
  North East Marine
  Engine Co, Sunderland:
  ihp not known

CATFORD

(1948) South Eastern Gas
  Board
2,724grt; 319ft 4in
  (97.32m) loa × 44ft
  (13.46m) beam
S.P. Austin & Son,
  Sunderland
Oil 4SA 6-cyl with SR
  gearing by Ruston &
  Hornsby, Lincoln: bhp
  not known

Moored on the buoys in the River Tyne with other coastal craft, waiting for a berth at the Harton Staiths on the South Shields side of the river, are the colliers *Mr Therm* and *Catford*, the former a steamship, the latter motor-driven. The view, taken in 1958, is looking in the direction of Tynemouth with the Smiths Dock Co premises at North Shields in the background beyond the funnel of a BP oil tanker. The small 1935-built, 214 gross ton bunkering tanker *BP Shipbuilder* appears to be tucked-in on the shoreward side of the *Catford*. Both colliers feature the buff-painted upperworks typical of this type of vessel. Note that they each have a unique number displayed above the bridge. This form of identification, allocated by the PLA Shipping Control Centre at Gravesend and illuminated at night, was used for the identification of passing vessels. The Harton Staiths, served by the nearby St Hilda colliery, were among a number of important coaling stations along the banks of the Tyne, including those at Dunston and Howden, all part of a major industry that had been in existence since the seventeenth century. The *Catford* was sold to Greek owners as the *Aispiros* in 1967, then going through a sequence of further name changes – *Zephyros* (1968), *Point Clear* (1969) and *Oliva* (1969) – until lost in an explosion and fire on 8 July 1971 while bound from Szczecin to Leith with a cargo of chemicals. All 18 crew members were rescued. The *Mr Therm*, originally owned by the Gas, Light & Coke Co, London was transferred to North Thames Gas Board ownership in 1950. She was removed from Lloyd's Register ten years later, most probably sold for scrapping.
Kenneth Wightman

JOHN ORWELL PHILLIPS

(2/1955) North Thames Gas Board
3,391grt; 339ft (103.32m) loa × 46ft 8in (14.22m) beam
W. Pickersgill & Sons, Sunderland
Triple expansion 3-cyl steam reciprocating by North East Marine Engine Co, Sunderland: 1,275ihp

Loading with coal at the Harton Staiths on 20 June 1956 is the collier *John Orwell Phillips*, sister to the *Frederick John Evans*. The gravity spouts of the elevators are lowered over her open midship holds. In attendance is the France Fenwick steam tug *Robert Redhead* (ex *Hannah Jolliffe*), built in 1900. During the 1960s and 1970s, with the commissioning of oil-fired and nuclear power stations, along with the transition from 'town' to 'natural' gas extracted from the North Sea, the number of colliers working the East Coast reduced drastically as the trade diminished. Many of the remaining colliers were adapted for carrying grain. Colliers typically featured broad hatches with high coamings and an absence, in most cases, of any shipboard cargo-handling gear. The majority, too, had self-trimming holds. They could complete the round trip from Newcastle to London in two to three days at 10½ knots, carrying as much as 3,000 tons of coal. Sold to Bovoyag Cia SA, Panama, in 1968 and renamed *Agios Fanourios*, the former *John Orwell Phillips* was involved in a collision with the Greek motor vessel *Epimelia* on the 16 April 1971 in the Fehmarnbelt, in the Baltic Sea. Though completely opened-up to the sea on her starboard side, the *Agios Fanourios* managed to reach Kiel for dry-docking. However, the damage was considered to be too extensive for repair and instead she was broken up at Nakskov, Denmark.
Kenneth Wightman

MANCUNIUM

(12/1946) North West Water Authority (Eastern Division)
1,378grt; 263ft (80.16m) loa × 38ft 2in (11.63) beam
Ferguson Bros Ltd, Port Glasgow
2 × Oil 4SA 6-cyl with Twiflex couplings and SR reverse gearing by Mirrlees National Ltd, Stockport: 1,420bhp

The distinctive Manchester-based effluents tanker *Mancunium*, seen outbound on the Mersey, has long, low lines and an elliptical counter stern. Formerly a steamer, she was re-engined with diesels in 1962. Her single lifeboat, supported in gravity davits, seems to be unusually located on the port side of the main deck working area. Beyond and to the right of the lifeboat may be seen the deck ventilators that were characteristic of this type of vessel. Like the already seen *Haweswater*, the *Mancunium* was a powerful, twin-screw vessel. The letters 'MC' displayed on the deck railings abaft her bridge were illuminated at night for easy identification by Manchester Ship Canal lock staff in much the same way as the PLA number system. Originally owned by the Rivers Department of the City of Manchester, she first transferred to the Middle Mersey Effluent Treatment Unit in 1974 and then passed to the North West Water Authority in 1977. Sold to Effluent Services Ltd in the summer of 1986, she then transferred to Southampton, working under charter for the Southern Water Authority. The *Mancunium* was broken up at Newport, South Wales, from January 1990. *Mick Lindsay*

Photographed passing under the Northam Bridge, Southampton, is the converted sand and gravel suction dredger *Steel Welder*. Her hopper hold is filled with gravel destined to be pumped ashore at a wharf further up the River Itchen for ultimate use either for land reclamation purposes or for a civil engineering project. Her suction dredging gear is stowed along the starboard side, supported by a single off-centre davit. She is so heavily laden that the main deck is almost awash. Formerly the Shell Mex & BP-owned tanker *Shell Welder*, she was extensively employed in Southampton Water in both capacities for both her original and subsequent owners. Her paintwork and general condition reflect the severe weathering and wear experienced by dredging craft of all types. *Mick Lindsay*

STEEL WELDER

(3/1955) ex *Shell Welder* (1974)
Northwood (Fareham) Ltd
500grt; 171ft (52.10m) loa × 29ft 8in (9.05m) beam
Clelands (Successors) Ltd, Wallsend-on-Tyne
Oil 2SA 6-cyl by Crossley Bros, Manchester: 570bhp

GALLIONS REACH

(1936) Port of London Authority
795grt; 188ft (53.30m) loa × 35ft 11in (10.95m) beam
H. Robb Ltd, Leith
Triple expansion 3-cyl steam reciprocating by C.D. Holmes & Co, Hull: 900ihp

The steam grab hopper dredger *Gallions Reach*, seen on the Thames near Tilbury in October 1966, heads for the open sea to dump her load of spoil. Two of her three cranes, all stowed in the rest position, are arranged athwartships across the broadest part of her hull while the third is located on the foredeck. Soon after she was sold to the North Sea & River Salvage Co, the *Gallions Reach* sank on the River Tees on 7 October 1971 after striking a submerged object off the entrance to the Furness Basin. The accident occurred while she was engaged in clearing silt in preparation for the fitting out of the ore-oil carrier *Tyne Bridge* which was to be launched three weeks later at the Swan Hunter yard at Haverton Hill. Extensively damaged, the *Gallions Reach* was raised and taken to dry dock where she was declared a constructive total loss. She was sold for breaking up locally.
Kenneth Wightman

ST. KATHERINE

(1928) Port of London
  Authority
337grt; 137ft 6in (41.90m)
  loa × 26ft 1in (7.95m)
  beam
Philips & Sons
  Shipbuilders, Dartmouth
Triple expansion 6-cyl
  steam reciprocating
  driving twin screws: ihp
  not known

The PLA yacht *St. Katherine* passes through the entrance lock into the King George V Dock, London, under the watchful eye of a Merchant Navy officer. The flag at the masthead is the PLA houseflag. At her ensign staff is what is known as a defaced Blue Ensign with an heraldic sealion supporter of the PLA coat of arms. Berthed ahead of her in the dock is one of the Royal Mail Line's passenger ships of the *Amazon* class. Although categorised as a steam yacht, the *St. Katherine* was in fact employed by the PLA as an inspection and hydrographic vessel. She also performed routine tours of inspections of the docks carrying PLA executives and groups of VIP passengers, probably such an event being depicted in this view. Her principal employment was in the production and maintenance of navigation charts published by her owners. Taken up by the Admiralty as an auxiliary yacht with the pennant number *4.56*, her wartime duties were with the 'examination' service until decommissioned in 1945. After a spell of service in the 1950s as a static floating 'office' in the St Katherine Docks, she was sold out of the PLA fleet. Since then the *St. Katherine* has survived as the floating platform for a sequence of Thames-side clubs and restaurants under the name 'The Yacht Club Limited'. Currently she is moored on the north embankment, near Temple Pier, functioning as a Thai Restaurant. *Kenneth Wightman*

JAMES PRIOR

(1963) ex *James P.* (1995) J.J. Prior (Transport) Ltd
191grt; 111ft 9in (34.06m) loa × 22ft 4in (6.80m) beam
J. Pollock, Sons & Co, Faversham
Oil 2SA 2-cyl by Skandiaverken A/B, Lysekil: bhp not
known

Pictured motoring past a large LPG tanker berthed, possibly at the Canvey Island terminal on the River Thames, is the small gravel barge *James Prior*, normally based at Ballast Quay, Fingringhoe, near Colchester. She has a carrying capacity of 280–290 tonnes. Note the high coamings to her hatches. Her crew's quarters are split between her forecastle and poop, the 'H'-shaped flue up forward probably serving her galley. Alongside it is the curved hatchway entrance to the accommodation area below – a claustrophobic space lacking any portholes. The *James Prior* was still in service in 2007 despite having had a quite catastrophic accident in September 2005 when she collided with Battersea Bridge, London. Wedged under the bridge with a fast-running tide, she extensively damaged the structure and had her wheelhouse, funnel and small signal mast demolished. Prior to 1995 she carried the shorter name *James P. Mick Lindsay*

RAMSGATE

(3/1962) District Council of Thanet, Ramsgate
168grt; 102ft (31.09m) loa × 26ft 8in (8.11m) beam
W. J. Yarwood & Sons Ltd, Northwich
Oil 4SA 8-cyl with SR reverse gear by L. Gardner &
Sons Ltd: 200bhp

The *Ramsgate* was launched on 15 February 1962 and when she entered service, in March 1962, she replaced a 1936-built steam-driven grab hopper/dredger of the same name. The function of the newer vessel was the same as her predecessor, namely to keep Ramsgate harbour dredged, but she was also permitted to operate at ports between Whitstable and Dover. A feature of the *Ramsgate* was that she had bottom doors for dumping sand and aggregate, or spoil, at sea. The undated photograph shows the *Ramsgate* in her home port with, to the right, the berthed Sally Freight ferry *Eurovoyager* ex *Prins Albert*. The *Ramsgate*'s crane is at rest with the grab stowed to the port of her hatch. *Mick Lindsay*

The *Lifeline* was originally built for the Admiralty and launched on 17 August 1943 as HMS *Lifeline* of the eleven-ship *Dispenser* class. She was commissioned in February 1944, during the latter stages of the Second World War, to serve as a salvage/boom defence vessel. As originally constructed she was single screw driven by a triple expansion engine, with massive bow sheaves and a heavy lift mast. As such she was classified as a Steam Coastal Salvage Vessel. From 1947 she was taken up for mercantile employment and in 1961, a year after she was listed as being for disposal, she was converted to diesel propulsion. In the early 1970s, Risdon Beazley, one of Britain's most successful private salvage companies, bought her along with a number of similar vessels from the Admiralty. They adapted her for further salvage service and in August 1978 she was transferred to Singapore for salvage work in the South China Sea. After working on the *Taigyo Maru*, a Japanese steamship that had been torpedoed off the coast of Malaya in February 1945, following which she was scrapped at Singapore in 1981. The photograph shows the refitted *Lifeline* alongside the then busy Southampton Town Quay in July 1975. Painted in a red lead livery, she is still sporting her massive sheaves. In the background can be seen the once prestigious Ocean Terminal, home terminus for Cunard White Star transatlantic liners, and to the left of the picture the RNR shore establishment, at HMS *Wessex*.
Ray Sprake

LIFELINE

(2/1944) Risdon Beazley
   Marine Ltd
752grt; 178ft 10in
   (54.51m) loa × 35ft 8in
   (10.88m) beam
Smith's Dock Co Ltd,
   South Bank,
   Middlesbrough
Oil 2SA 4-cyl by British
   Polar Engines, Glasgow:
   640bhp

LESRIX

(11/1957) ex *Whitehaven*
(1964) J.R. Rix & Sons
676grt; 185ft (56.38m) loa
× 32ft 8in (9.95m)
beam
Jos. L. Meyer, Papenburg
Oil 4SA 6-cyl by
Klöckner-Humboldt-
Deutz, Cologne: 755bhp

A crystal-clear, early-morning view of a smart general bulk cargo coaster, the *Lesrix* was photographed in 1974 berthed it is believed at Whitehaven, Cumbria. Her MacGregor hatch covers are in the open position ready to work cargo. Note how the hatch sections are larger on her well deck hold and smaller on the more spacious quarterdeck hold. It always seems that something unusual may be seen on deck or hanging over the side of small coasters – in this case a red oil drum at the port stern quarter for ship's trash! Built originally for Whitehaven Shipping Co, the *Lesrix* served J. R. Rix & Co of Hull from 1964 to 1986 when she was sold and renamed *Nan 1*. In 1992 her name was changed again to *Chada* and a year later she became the *Shaman 1*. Finally, in 1994, traded to Syrian-flag owners she was given the name *Urouba 1*. She was broken up in Romania in June 2004.
Mick Lindsay

TILLERMAN

(1/1963) C. Rowbotham &
Sons (Management) Ltd
807grt; 203ft 1in (61.88m)
loa × 30ft 9in (9.38m)
beam
Drypool Engineering &
Drydock Co, Hull
Vee Oil 2SA 12-cyl (by
builder): 900bhp

Photographed off Cowes, Isle of Wight, in June 1978, the coastal tanker *Tillerman* heads out into the Solent after a call in the River Medina. Small craft in the estuary, through which she is being navigated, constitute a particular hazard to coastal shipping particularly in foggy conditions or in darkness. Like so many coastal vessels, after their days with British owners had ended, the *Tillerman* went through a sequence of changes of ownership and name after Rowbothams disposed of her in 1986: *Ohoud* (1986), *Al Amin* (1987), *Flying Trader* (1990) and *Al Mahroukat Al Awal* (1991), remaining in Middle Eastern waters throughout this period of her career. Her subsequent fate is not known by the authors. *Mick Lindsay*

LEADSMAN

(10/1968) C. Rowbotham
& Sons (Management)
Ltd
843grt; 205ft (62.48m) loa
× 32ft 9in (9.98m)
beam
Drypool Engineering &
Drydock Co, Hull
Vee Oil 2SA 12-cyl (by
builder): 1,120bhp

A later Rowbotham tanker, the *Leadsman* is seen off Swansea in late May 1981. Four years after the photograph was taken she was sold to Effluent Services Ltd, London, and renamed *Alston*. In 1997 she was sold for a second time, becoming the *Als* of Hydria I. Maritime, Piraeus, a year later moving on again, to become the *Irini*. It is understood that she may still be actively employed. *Mick Lindsay*

GLEN STRATHALLAN

(1928) King Edward VII Nautical College/Shaftsbury Homes & Arethusa Society
330grt; 139ft 2in (42.41m) loa × 24ft 1in (7.34m) beam
Cochrane & Sons, Selby
Triple expansion 3-cyl steam reciprocating driving single screw by C.D. Holmes, Hull: ihp not known

Ordered as a 690 ton steam trawler, the *Glen Strathallan* was purchased by the millionaire R.A. Colby Cubbin prior to completion, after the company which had ordered her went bankrupt. Fitted out as a luxury yacht, she was loaned to the Royal Navy during the Second World War, serving as an escort vessel. Later, she became an anti-submarine yacht in service with the Royal Canadian Navy with the pennant number *FY.010* until returned in 1945. Following the untimely death of her philanthropic patron in 1955, she was bequeathed to the King Edward VII Nautical College for service as a training ship for Merchant Navy officers. She is seen here on the Thames in that role, passing what is thought to be Beckton gas works where a collier is discharging alongside the wharf. When the *Glen Strathallan*'s training duties came to an end she was scuttled outside Plymouth Sound on 27 April 1970 to act as a diver training wreck site. Her engines were removed and are preserved at the Science Museum. *Kenneth Wightman*

HAMBLE

(4/1964) Shell Mex & BP
Ltd
1,182grt; 214ft 10in
(65.48m) loa × 37ft 3in
(11.35m) beam
Henry Robb Ltd, Leith
Oil 2SA 6-cyl by British
Polar Engines, Glasgow:
1,230bhp

The *Hamble* and her sister the *Killingholme* (see *BP Scorcher, page 7*) were built to carry three non-kindred products simultaneously. They were each manned by 14 crew members. When she entered service the *Hamble*'s deadweight of 1,487 tons gave her the largest carrying capacity in the company's coastal fleet at the time. She was employed in transporting refined oil products around the British Isles to coastal depots for onward distribution. Her entry into service heralded the withdrawal of the five 1921-built steam-driven coasters that were still in the fleet. In 1976 BP and Shell ended their joint distribution venture and the *Hamble* passed to Shell Oil, renamed *Shell Refiner* from 1979. In 1981 she was sold and renamed *Metro Star* and in 1982 she was lengthened and deepened, to 274ft 7in (83.70m) and 26ft 3in (7.98m) respectively. She was sold in 1987 and renamed *Erin T* and again in 1992 as the *Marine Supplier*. Viewed alongside at Workington in Cumbria during July 1975, the *Hamble* appears to have discharged her cargo and there seems to be little activity. The coastal trade supported by tankers like the *Hamble* formed much of the lifeblood of small ports like Workington. *Mick Lindsay*

DUBLIN

(4/1969) Shell Mex & BP Ltd
1,077grt; 214ft 10in (65.48m) loa × 37ft 2in (11.33m) beam
Hall, Russell & Co Ltd, Aberdeen
Oil 2SA 8-cyl by British Polar Engines, Glasgow: 1,200bhp

The *Dublin*, launched on 4 December 1968, was one of a number of coastal tankers that joined the Shell Mex & BP fleet in the 1960s. Named after ports in the British Isles to which they traded, the new nomenclature temporarily phased out the former *BP* and *Shell* prefixes. She had a deadweight tonnage of 1,537 on a draught of 14 feet 7 inches and was capable of a speed of 11 knots. Following the termination of the joint distribution venture between BP and Shell Mex in 1976, the *Dublin* passed to the new BP Oil concern and was renamed *BP Springer*. She was renamed *Border Springer* in 1997. After a further seven years of trading she arrived at Santander on 26 October 2004 to be scrapped. This undated photograph of the *Dublin* shows her alongside, possibly at Grangemouth, looking remarkably pristine in a light condition ready for loading. Moored aft of her is another coastal tanker, the already-loaded *Lone Wonsild*. *Mick Lindsay*

SAND LARK

(10/1963) South Coast Shipping Co Ltd
540grt; 174ft 1in (53.07m) loa × 30ft 4in
(9.25m) beam
J. Bolson & Son Ltd, Poole
Oil 4SA 6-cyl with flexilbe coupling & SR
reverse gearing by Lister Blackstone
Marine Ltd, Dursley: 495bhp

When the *Sand Lark* entered service in 1963, she was a modified version of the *Sand Snipe* and *Sand Grebe* that had preceeded her from the same shipyard. She was followed a year later by the *Sand Gull* and *Sand Tern*. Along with her sisters and others of the fleet she was immediately employed in the carriage of aggregates for the building of the 600 MW power station being built at Fawley in the early 1960s – a lucrative contract. She was a regular caller at Southampton's Itchen Quays and the then busy Town Quay. In 1991 she was sold and renamed *Sand Martin*. She was sold to Sunward Shipping Ltd of St Vincent & the Grenadines but by 2002 she had disappeared from Lloyd's Register under this name. The *Sand Lark* is seen here moored alongside in her home port of Southampton during July 1981. A good close-up of her in light loaded condition, her continuous employment has left her hull shabby and rust-streaked. *Mick Lindsay*

SAND GULL

(12/1964) South Coast Shipping Co Ltd
534grt; 173ft 11in (53.01m) loa × 30ft 4in(9.25m) beam
J. Bolson & Son Ltd, Poole
Oil 4SA 6-cyl with flexible coupling & SR reverse gear
by Blackstone & Co Ltd, Stamford: 495bhp

Built as a sister to the *Sand Lark,* and *Sand Tern,* the *Sand Gull* joined a fleet of nine other vessels. She was designed as a sand suction dredger in which sand and aggregate used for the construction industry were drawn from the seabed and deposited in her single hold. A deadweight capacity of 675 tons could be handled. Not long after she entered service she was employed in discharging aggregates at Fawley for the construction of the Fawley power station. She grounded near Ventnor, Isle of Wight on 12 August 1992, was refloated but only to be beached on 16 August. She was again refloated and towed to Southampton on 18 August. She was moved to Marchwood on 11 October 1992 and later scrapped. The *Sand Gull* was photographed in August 1988 alongside at one of her regular ports, Poole Harbour. With the crane and grab that are adjacent to her, she is probably completing her discharge of sand or ballast. Her suction equipment is stowed to her starboard side. *Mick Lindsay*

(12/1952) Stephenson Clarke Ltd
1,570grt; 240ft 10in (73.41m) loa × 37ft 9in (11.51m) beam
Grangemouth Dockyard Co Ltd, Grangemouth
Oil 2SA 8-cyl by British Polar Engines, Glasgow: 1,500bhp

The *Totland* was launched on 23 September 1952 and three months later joined a growing fleet of motor- and steam-driven colliers. Like most of the vessels in the Stephenson Clarke fleet, she was designed for the carriage of coal to power stations and other installations with shore-side discharging gear. With a service speed of 11½ knots she was the fastest ship in the fleet at the time. Under Stephenson Clarke's usual system of nomenclature, vessels were named after Sussex villages; thus, the *Totland*, along with the *Gosport*, *Emsworth* and *Portsmouth* bucked the established trend. By 1972 the company fleet had grown to around 36 ships. The *Totland*'s large deadweight tonnage of 2,008 made her attractive to other operators and she was sold in 1974 to Panamanian buyers and renamed *Astroland*. By 1975 she had become the Cypriot-owned *Ivy* before being sold to Greek owners in 1976 and renamed *Agios Fanourios V*. She was sold on again in 1981 as the *Eftichia* and broken up in 1986. This seemingly austere photograph, taken on 6 June 1956, shows the *Totland* outward bound from North Shields. Her ochre upperworks and shorter motorship funnel are very distinctive. Of interest, moored in the river, is what may well be one of the vast fleet of Aberdeen trawlers then operational, the *A118*. *Kenneth Wightman*

MASSYS

(10/1952) ex *Sanastasia* (1973) ex *Gosport* (1972)
Blue Pilots Navigation Co Ltd, Cyprus
1,820grt; 262ft (79.86 m) loa × 38ft 9in (11.81m) beam
S. P. Austin & Son Ltd, Sunderland
Oil 2SA 8-cyl by Sulzer Bros, Winterthur: 1,150bhp

Launched on 23 April 1952, the *Gosport* entered service with Stephenson Clarke two months before the *Totland* (see previous page). She had a deadweight capacity of 2,395 tons. By 1972 a lot of the smaller coastal coal-fired power stations were being phased out in favour of major ones fuelled by pulverised coal dust or oil. Thus, the *Gosport* was sold that year and renamed *Sanastasia* for Cypriot owners. The following year saw her sold again within Cyprus when she was renamed *Massys*, adapted for the carriage of general cargo. On 7 December 1977, whilst off the coast of Guinea, she caught fire after an engine room explosion and sank in position 9°14'N, 14°58'W. She had been bound for Conakry and Lagos from Bulgaria. Moored alongside at Avonmouth on 21 October 1974, the photograph shows the Cypriot *Massys* still trading after 22 years. Although she looks clean and bright in her new owner's livery featuring white upperworks, a style adopted later by Stephenson Clarke, her design betrays her former origins as a British coastal collier. *Mick Lindsay*

BRAMBER

(6/1954) ex *Greenbatt* (1960) Stephenson Clarke Ltd
1,968grt; 264ft 11in (80.75m) loa × 40ft 3in (12.27m) beam
S. P. Austin & Son Ltd, Sunderland
Triple Expansion 3-cyl steam reciprocating by North Eastern Marine Eng. Co, Sunderland: ihp not known

The *Bramber* was originally launched on 31 March 1954 as the *Greenbatt* for Newbigin Steam Shipping Co of Newcastle. To meet Stephenson Clarke's growing demand for colliers she was sold to them in 1960 and became the *Bramber*. Although she had a deadweight capacity of 2,480 tons her service speed of 9¹/₂ knots made her the slowest ship in the company. This along with her steam reciprocating machinery may have influenced the company's decision to dispose of her after only eight years service. She was sold to Maldives Shipping Co of Ceylon in 1968 and renamed *Maldive Sailor*. She was later broken up at Gadani Beach, Pakistan, commencing January 1975. In this undated photograph, the *Bramber* is moored off Tilbury power station in a fully laden condition. Her MacGregor hatches are rolled back ready for her to go alongside the power station jetty and discharge her cargo of coal. *Kenneth Wightman*

SHOREHAM

(2/1957)
   Stephenson Clarke Ltd
1,834grt; 242ft (73.76m)
   loa × 40ft 2in (12.24m)
   beam
Hall, Russell & Co Ltd,
   Aberdeen
Oil 2SA 8-cyl by Sulzer
   Bros, Winterthur:
   1,225bhp

HERON

(5/1957) General Steam
   Navigation Co (GSNCo)
943grt 232ft 6in (70.87m)
   loa × 37ft 7in (11.46m)
   beam
C. Hill & Sons Ltd, Bristol
Oil 2 SA 8-cyl by British
   Polar Engines, Glasgow:
   1,280bhp

The *Shoreham* is moored forward of GSNCo's *Heron* in this photograph of them taken together in November 1967 alongside 101 berth in Southampton's Western Docks. The *Shoreham* was launched on 22 August 1956 and joined Stephenson Clarke as one of the fastest colliers in the fleet with a speed of 12 knots. Like others in the fleet she was designed with a deadweight tonnage of 2,350 for the carriage of coal to power stations and down-river gas works. During 1969 she was lengthened by 20ft (6.10m) which increased her gross and deadweight tonnages to 1,950 and 2,754 respectively. She must have proved an economical vessel as she spent 22 years in service with Stephenson Clarke before being scrapped at Strood in September 1979. The *Heron* was launched on 15 November 1956 as an open shelter deck general cargo vessel. When she joined the GSNCo fleet in 1957 she was one of a group of similarly designed ships, others being the *Gannet*, *Grebe*, *Sandpiper* and *Woodlark*. She had a deadweight capacity of around 895 tons which included some refrigerated cargo space, and she was mainly employed on routes between London and continental ports. The *Heron* was sold out of the company in 1970. *Mick Lindsay*

PULBOROUGH

(4/1965) Stephenson Clarke Ltd
4,995grt; 369ft 11in (112.76m) bp × 53ft 6in (16.31m) beam
Blyth Shipbuilding & Drydock Co Ltd, Blyth
Oil 2SA 9-cyl by British Polar Engines, Glasgow: 2,600bhp

When the *Pulborough* entered service with the company in 1965 she was the largest and longest ship to join the fleet since the end of the Second World War and the fourth ship to bear the name. Launched on 17 December 1964, she had a deadweight tonnage of 7,665. She was joined two years later by a sister ship, the *Rogate*, which replaced an earlier vessel of the same name. For the *Pulborough*, her owners returned to British Polar Engines for her propulsion plant. The *Pulborough* gave Stephenson Clarke 21 years of service before she arrived at Gadani Beach, Pakistan, on 22 September 1986 for scrapping. She is seen here photographed at an unidentified locality during October 1975. Note how the two-island design of the earlier colliers of the company has been replaced by a single accommodation block aft and the extension of the foredeck; also, the change of upperworks to white, with the addition of the houseflag in a shield motif added to the bow. *Mick Lindsay*

ISLAND EXPLORER

(1949) ex *Deneb* (1975) Tracom Overseas Ltd
492grt; 139ft 1in (42.40m) loa × 26ft 4in (8.03m) beam
Arnhemsche Stoom. Maats, Arnhem
Oil 2SA 8-cyl by Gebr. Stork NV, Hengelo: 700bhp

This interesting vessel was originally built for The Netherlands' equivalent of Trinity House, the Loodswezen (then a division of the Dutch Ministry of Defence), for service as a pilot cutter under the name *Deneb* in the approaches to the Rivers Scheldt and Rhine. She was one of two similar vessels, the other being the *Sirius*, which was acquired by Greenpeace in 1981. Here as the *Island Explorer*, the former *Deneb* is photographed alongside Shepards Wharf in Cowes harbour during August 1976, after conversion into a coastal research and survey vessel for the offshore drilling industry. Below her bridge may be seen the badge of her former company. Beyond her bow can be seen the Cowes Floating Bridge No. 4 on the slipway of the Clare Lallow boatyard, undergoing annual maintenance. *Mick Lindsay*

Built to a design heavily-influenced by Admiralty thinking, the buoy and lighthouse tender *Ready* was one of a class of three ships, the others being the *Vestal* and *Argus*. They were the largest ships to be owned by Trinity House until the advent of the third *Patricia* in 1982. To minimise construction costs, the trio were fitted with war-surplus steam engines but with their high fuel consumption, over time this made them too expensive to run. The *Ready* was one of four tenders based at Harwich, Essex. She was broken up at Grays, Essex, commencing 20 April 1978, having been laid up in reserve the previous year. In this view of her, taken at Southampton in July 1973, she is flying the alphabetical flags 'R' and 'Y' above her bridge, indicating that she is not under way but is dragging her anchor. *Mick Lindsay*

READY

(10/1947) Corporation of Trinity House
1,920grt; 266ft (81.07m) loa × 40ft (12.19m) beam
Blyth Drydock Co, Cowpen Quay, Blyth
Triple expansion 6-cyl steam reciprocating driving twin screws by Geo. Clark Ltd, Sunderland: 2,084ihp

MERMAID

(1959) Corporation of Trinity House
1,425grt; 221ft (67.36m) loa × 38ft (11.58m) beam
J. Samuel White & Co, Cowes, Isle of Wight
4 × Oil 4SA 6-cyl connected via 4 generators and 2
electric motors by English Electric Co, Preston, to twin
screws: 1,450shp

By the early 1960s, Trinity House needed a fleet of nine ships minimum to maintain its full range of duties and responsibilities and, in preparation, it ordered four new twin-screw tenders from the J. Samuel White shipyard on the Isle of Wight, the lead ship being the *Mermaid*, shown here. In this class, diesel-electric propulsion was adopted in preference to steam plant. Though smaller than the *Ready* trio, their capabilities were comparable: they could accommodate 10 light officers and 21 lightsmen during reliefs, their 15 ton derrick permitted them to lift the largest buoys while their towing winch was powerful enough to tow all light vessels then in service. Stationed initially at Great Yarmouth, covering a district that extended from the Scottish border to Southwold, Suffolk, she was later transferred to Harwich. The *Mermaid* was sold by Trinity House to Greek owners in 1986 and renamed *City of Athens*. The same year she was sold again to Transocean Management (Lauriston) Ltd, Gibraltar, becoming the *Red Rose*. She was broken up at Aliaga, Spain, in August 1995. *Don Smith*

WINSTON CHURCHILL

(5/1963) Corporation of Trinity House
1,451grt; 222ft 2in (67.7m) loa × 37ft 6in (11.5m) beam
J. Samuel White & Co, Cowes, Isle of Wight
4 × Oil 4SA 6-cyl connected via 4 generators and 2 electric motors by English Electric Co, Preston, to twin screws: 1,450shp

Fourth ship of the *Mermaid*-class, the *Winston Churchill*, named in honour of the Corporation's most celebrated Elder Brother for over half a century, was slightly different from her earlier class mates, the other two of the quartet being the *Siren* and *Stella*. Her accommodation structure was enclosed at the boat deck level and her bridge extended across her full beam. The *Winston Churchill* was photographed at the East Cowes depot in August 1967. Beyond her foredeck can be seen the Red Funnel car ferry *Cowes Castle*. Like her sisters, the *Winston Churchill* was later modified, having a helicopter landing pad fitted aft requiring the repositioning of the mainmast. After Trinity House disposed of her in 1989 to Christopher A. Craft, she was sold again to Noble Shipping Ltd in 1993. Thereafter, she was supposedly converted into a private yacht. However, in the June 2002 issue of the World Ship Society journal *Marine News* she appeared laid up at Phuket, Thailand, in a rusty condition and with her name shortened to *Churchill*. *David Williams*

CITY OF SOUTHAMPTON

(9/1969) ex *Hoveringham V* (1989)
United Marine Aggregates
1,027grt; 236ft 3in (72.00m) loa × 39ft 8in (12.10m) beam
Appledore Shipbuilding Co, Appledore
Vee Oil 4SA 8-cyl by English Electric Diesels, Ruston Eng. Div, Lincoln: 1,050bhp

A sand suction hopper dredger, one of an identical pair completed late in the 1960s, the *City of Southampton* entered service under the name *Hoveringham V* for Hoveringham Gravels Ltd, Hull. As built, she measured 879 gross tons on a hull length of 208ft 3in (63.50m) but in 1973 she was lengthened to the dimensions and tonnage stated above. Fifteen years later she passed to new owners, United Marine Aggregates, remaining with them until 1997 when she was disposed of to become the *Leon I*. A year later she was renamed again, as the *Kavonissi*. The *City of Southampton* was photographed at Newport, South Wales on 18 June 1989, shortly after joining United Marine Aggregates. *Mick Lindsay*

CLEARWAY

(3/1927) Workington Docks
& Harbour Board
276grt; 115ft 1in (35.08m)
loa × 27ft 1in (8.26m)
beam
Hall & Co, Aberdeen
Triple expansion 3-cyl
steam reciprocating (by
builder): 300ihp

Commissioned as a self-discharging grab hopper dredger to keep the channels and berths at Whitehaven on the Solway Firth clear of silt, the appropriately named *Clearway* was launched on 25 January 1927 and entered service for the Whitehaven Harbour Commissioners less than two months later. Whitehaven's trades of coal, methane, cement, grain, timber and chemicals depended vitally on the maintenance of sufficient depth of water for safe navigation for a range of calling coastal vessels and the *Clearway* continued with her duties at the Cumbrian port for over half a century, interrupted only by war service on the Clyde and occasional surveys and overhauls on the slipway at Ramsay. She performed similar duties for the nearby Workington Docks & Harbour Board, later coming under the ownership of that port authority. She is seen here berthed alongside one of the commercial quays at Whitehaven. Though a veteran by the time this photograph was taken, her characteristic steamship look is clearly evident and she remains in a smart condition. Withdrawn from service in 1992 at the time when phosphate rock shipments into Whitehaven ceased, she remained idle for five years while attempts were made to find alternative employment or a preservation group willing to take her on. Sadly, this was not to be and in 1997 she was towed to Millom for breaking up. The *Clearway* had remained coal-fired throughout her life and, prior to her disposal, was one of the few vessels so fuelled still in existence. *Mick Lindsay*

COEDMOR

(6/1946) ex *Arran Monarch* (1964) ex *VIC 57* (1948)
David G. & Christine J. Williams (see below)
181grt; 107ft 9in (32.84m) loa × 20ft (6.10m) beam
J. Pollock Sons & Co Ltd, Faversham
Oil 4SA 6-cyl by Bergius-Kelvin Co Ltd, Glasgow: 160bhp

Displaying the typical lines of a former Admiralty VIC lighter, the *Coedmor*, registered in Llanelli, was in fact a small sand dredger having been converted in 1965, a year after being lengthened by 27ft (8.23m). As completed she had been fitted with steam reciprocating machinery. After just two years with the Ministry of Transport, she was sold privately to P. M. Herbert of Bude and renamed *Arran Monarch*. Later, in 1964, she was acquired by Burry Sand Co Ltd, Llanelli, as the *Coedmor*. Her owners at the time of this undated photograph are not certain as she had a succession of Llanelli-based owners: Hollacombe Aggregates Ltd, D.G. & C.J. Williams and DGW Sand Co Ltd. The location of the photograph is the Camel estuary at Padstow, Cornwall. The flat-bottomed *Coedmor*, with a 244 deadweight tons capacity, was employed over many years dredging for sand along this stretch of the Cornish coast, continuing until the late 1990s. She was eventually dismantled alongside the North Quay at Hayle, near St Ives.
Mick Lindsay